The Bel Canto Buzz

Beautiful Singing Made Simple!

by

Debra Lynn

Illustrations by Sally Foster
Cover design by Ken Martin

Third edition

ISBN-13: 978-1-4752-2969-1
ISBN-10: 1-4752-2969-0

http://www.debralynnmusic.com

Table of Contents

Foreword

I first heard Deb when we were both part of the Sayegh Garcia Marchesi vocal studio in San Francisco, California. I remember to this day the way my head turned to see where this amazingly clear and beautiful voice was coming from. If memory serves she was singing *O Luce di quest anima*. Her golden notes and sound drew me in along with her compelling stature and eyes. "Ah!" I thought, "Another fabulously intense and interesting person!" Afterwards, a tea shared with lemon and honey solidified the beginning of a long, warm friendship together.

During our shared training experience, in addition to having a stellar set of pipes and natural expression, Deb always led the way with deep personal integrity for the work with which she was involved. Everything about her was not only the best she could be, but also easy and fun for whoever was involved.

Deb's choice to include teaching voice along with her active concert performing is no surprise. Her love for people and dedication to vocal beauty make her a natural for sharing what she has learned. Her success in teaching, along with the dedication, love and growth, which her students experience, in all fairness, should not be considered stop-the-press-news. A wonderful person, highly skilled, as well as a great communicator, it would be more surprising if she wasn't successful.

With her intelligence and general sense of ease and goodwill towards others suffusing the pages of her new book, *The Bel Canto Buzz* should delight readers who are interested in singing better, new voice teachers looking for ways to reach their students more effectively, as well as more experienced teachers who want a review of *bel canto* principles or to borrow some of her suggestions to use in their own studios. Deb's writing is fresh, understandable and clear—something, which is not always easily accomplished in the vocal academic world.

After reading through the sections, I found it easy to stand next to my piano (with mirror!), try out the suggestions, and experience changes almost instantly for myself.

I hope you enjoy the book as much as I did!

-Kate Michaels, Basel, Switzerland
Singer, actor, educator: www.katemichaels.com

Introduction

Why did I write this book?
One day, I experienced effortless singing.

It was so easy, in fact, that I felt nothing but complete control. I had been singing an Italian exercise at the time (where else—in the shower). For what had seemed like an eternity to that point, despite having an undergraduate degree in voice performance, twenty years of lessons from six prominent teachers and an enormous financial investment in my journey, I had been struggling to sing well.

And suddenly there I was, transforming from amateur to professional, in a light-bulb illuminating moment of understanding.

Many of us struggle to sing with ease. Yet we remain fascinated by those who DO seem to possess the "secret" to powerful, effortless pitch-perfect singing, as the popularity of several reality television shows attests to. It seems our very souls want to sing.

I have been given insight into this secret, which holds the ability to free your voice. I call it *The Bel Canto Buzz*. This area, when energized, has the capacity to completely stabilize your singing, while helping you remain better tuned and more accurate in your diction and phrasing. We're going to find this spot together, exercise it and start you on your journey to effortless singing.

Here's the key: what if I were to tell you that most of the challenges you've been having with your own singing have to do with the way you talk? It is the piece of the vocal puzzle that is completely overlooked in mainstream music education. After thousands of lessons, I had never heard a single instructor mention that the language I spoke was my primary problem—and yet, now I know that, clearly, it had been.

So, from the moment I felt that effortless tone emerge from my body, it became my fervent desire to share this understanding with anyone who had been challenged in one way or another with their own singing.

I will take it one step further: I now know that everyone can sing—and sing well. Now, after almost twenty years of teaching voice myself, I can attest to the fact that every single person that has crossed my studio's threshold has left an hour later knowing without a doubt that he or she could in fact sing with ease. So, together, we're going to unravel the difficulty most Americans or English-based speakers face when we try to sing. These challenges also extend to singing in other languages where the vowel structure causes the voice to resonate some of the sounds too far back in the mouth, close down at the ends of individual syllables or force the tongue to articulate consonants farther back on the hard palate.

First, we will need to understand what singing is: it's simply elongated vowel sounds. Next, we will discover that we're built like an instrument, physically designed to vibrate or resonate sound. Once you have these concepts down, it becomes a question of focusing the mind, stabilizing the muscles associated with singing, and establishing the Buzz.

As I discovered the secret to ease within my own body, through the benefits of the Italian language, I started to notice another group of singers who seemed to be creating effortless sound themselves—the Hawaiians. At the time, I had been living on Maui and was sitting in a restaurant listening to music sung by a joyful and radiant musician, singing in his native language. There was no strain; no aspects of his vocal range seemed to create any challenge for him. I asked him later if he had ever studied voice, and he replied, "No."

I then put two and two together. The Hawaiian language was put into written form by using the Italian/Latin language as the basis for phonetic translation, the two languages being related through their vowel structure. Both are considered pure vowel languages, unlike English. This forward, pure vowel component becomes key. Believe it or not, these Italian and Hawaiian vowels live in one spot in your mouth, this place I call the Buzz. When I help you to understand how to find and feel this place, your singing will be transformed.

My last teacher was a master of *bel canto*, beautiful singing. It is the time-honored fundamental Italianate understanding that was the standard of vocal production from 1800 to 1840. Lost to all but a few, via a lineage of teachers directly descended from Manuel Garcia, I am blessed to have had such a teacher. His steadfast work with me, high standard of excellence and consistent vocal practices also imbued in me the skill of deep, attentive listening, which facilitates my own ability to guide and empower others to unlock their voices.

The impact of my awareness and understanding humbles me, for although my own singing may bring joy to others for a few moments my ability to teach others how to sing with ease is what fills my heart with purpose and meaning.

Too many people in this world believe that they cannot sing well. This is not truth. This is a misunderstanding, a lack of clarity about how singing works and the challenges we all face. As an example, Americanized-English is a language that will not stay in tune by itself. Unless you are trained (or are very lucky), our language-based issues create more problems than you realize.

Come into my world for a little while and I will share with you tools and tips that will transform your life as a singer, and bring you and those you sing for endless hours of joy! Let's go find our Bel Canto Buzz!

Chapter 1: Everyone Can Sing! (This Might Surprise You)

Chapter 1: Everyone Can Sing! (This Might Surprise You)

Did You Know You Are Built Like a Stereo Speaker?

Most who struggle to sing with ease don't realize that humans are actually built to sing and that our bodies are designed like a high-end stereo speaker. If you have ever taken off the face of a stereo speaker and looked at its internal structure, you may recall seeing three cone-like structures on the wall of the speaker referred to as woofers, tweeters and mids; the cones are concave and respectively large, small and medium in size. When sound is made it sets up a vibration or sound wave. Each of these cones vibrates when sound is put through the speaker, and the sound is amplified. The larger cone amplifies the lowest notes and the smallest cone helps resonate the highest pitches or tones.

If you put your hand on your chest and hum a very low pitch, you will feel a vibration. Hum a note a bit higher and place your hand on your throat. Once again you will feel a vibration in that part of the body. If you hum a high note and place your fingers along the sides of your nose, you will feel another tiny vibration. So the lungs, throat and sinus area are all parts of the body in which we resonate sound. These are predominantly open areas of our musculature, where air passes through with ease.

Like the stereo speaker, the larger area —the lungs — predominantly amplifies the low notes, just like a woofer or the bass on a speaker. The throat resonates most of the middle register vibrations and, of course, the sinuses and bones of the face help resonate the highest notes we sing. As we get used to feeling the vibration of our tones and start to sing in a more balanced way, all of the resonators in our body work together to amplify our voices.

Our Mouths Form a Mini Amphitheater

Now, if we look at the vocal mechanism itself in its simplest form, it is referred to as the larynx. The vocal cords are only a very small part of this mechanism. They are part of this complex structure made up of cartilage, muscles, and even one bone—the hyoid—the only bone in the body that is not connected to any other bone. The main function of the larynx is to protect the airway. Speaking and making beautiful singing sounds is just a rather amazing bonus.

As our brain hears a tone, it sends a signal to the chords to create a note. As we inhale, the preparation that the pharynx makes towards the back of the throat, where we 'feel' the shaping, if you will, of the vowels, gets us prepared for articulation. As gentle air pressure is established with the vocal folds, they oscillate and produce a pitch or tone. That tone moves up into the throat, on that very thin stream of breath and energy. Once a vowel is articulated with a corresponding consonant, it is directed into the mouth where with sustained musculature, like the stable soundboard of a violin or guitar, our voice resonates and is heard outside our body.

If you have ever been to an outdoor concert for a band or orchestra, you may have seen a rounded structure on the stage behind the group playing. In Honolulu for example, the Waikiki Shell is just such an amphitheater, and it actually looks like a big seashell. This kind of shape behind an orchestra helps to amplify the sound and project it out towards the audience.

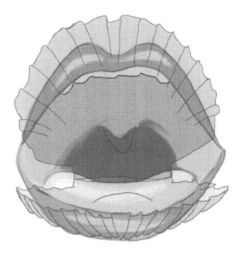

The inside of our mouth is designed like a mini-amphitheater. If you open your mouth pretty wide and inhale, you will notice the tongue sort of goes down and the roof of the mouth goes up. The back of the throat is like the curve of the shell. As sound comes up from the vocal cords combined with articulation, it can literally roll right over the roof of the mouth and be directed to exit by the teeth and lips. When executed properly, this coordinated action of thinking and creating a tone, articulating a consonant and vowel, directing, resonating and sustaining a sound happens in a split second.

Once we begin to really feel our voices inside our bodies and notice how the musculature placed into the proper position supports our singing, we will have an easier time resonating sound that the world can hear. Many teachers make the mistake of telling students to get the sound out or project louder, which typically causes singers to yell or force the sound. Believe it or not, as soon as we start to push or force our voices, the sound stops resonating properly and it will often feel as if it actually collapses. Too much airflow through the vocal cords without maintaining proper, gentle air pressure diffuses the tone, and in bel canto also destabilizes our *legato* or connected line.

As a side note, if our mind thinks we don't know what we are doing, we will tend to try to make sound happen in any way we can, which usually involves pressing the voice too hard or pushing too much air through the mechanism. Just know that this is a natural reaction to trying to figure out how to do something, when we have not been given any direction otherwise, reminiscent of the Jean Luke Picard *Star Trek* directive, "Make it so!"

This is especially true when working with children. Many voice teachers won't take young students, so they don't often get effective direction. But the reality is that most kids sing all the time and tend to yell and push regularly. One twelve-year-old that was brought to me for assistance had almost destroyed her ability to sing, as sections of her vocal range were completely missing. It took six months of reinforcing gentle tones and teaching her basic support principles to help guide her voice back to health, where she had a full range of notes available to her again, instead of the four or five notes she could sing for me initially. So, in my experience gently teaching children good singing habits early helps them develop healthy singing voices, as they grow into their instruments.

Now as adults, if we get used to placing the muscles in the right position, feeling how our voices vibrate and start playing with our vowel production for a while, our voices will begin to resonate properly and become louder naturally without pushing or yelling. We essentially become our own amplifier!

The Buzz: It Was Right Under Your Nose All the Time!

Believe it or not, how we think about directing and sustaining the sound coming out of us has everything to do with making the whole thing work. Our Americanized-English language's natural propensity is to sit or resonate way back in our mouths and throats. As a result of this, our singing often sounds swallowed or covered, like there's a little garage door darkening and dulling the sound.

By imitating the animated nature of Italian speech, we come close to feeling where this mysterious Buzz lives. If you think about someone you know who is Italian, you may recognize that the way they articulate and speak is somewhat more energetic and lifted than your own. By taking on these muscular mannerisms, we will feel a different brightness to the sounds we make. This will impact our tuning, as we combat the natural sagging that occurs in our English language.

If you draw a line across your face right under nose, this is the area where the forward vowels vibrate. If you hum an M for a moment with your lips closed, you may notice a feeling of vibration. If you make a mischievous little smile and hum again, you may start to notice the vibration moving up under your nose. This place where you are feeling a small vibration, is where the Buzz lives.

Another way to isolate this spot is to place your fingers like a moustache right under your nose, feeling the indentation between your gum line and cheekbones. Press gently into that space. Now, lift your cheek muscles up off the gum line right beside your nose. It will feel rather fake and if you start speaking, kind of makes you sound like you are from a foreign country. These lifted, engaged cheeks become important as we begin to stabilize our forward vowel placement and energized sound.

One warm-up I use to exercise this area is humming up and back by half steps in your lower register or chest voice. As we do this exercise, we start to bring our awareness to the Buzz. Just doing this one exercise begins to isolate and stabilize the positive vibration that will eventually make your voice sound even and well tuned.

Doing some general humming around the house while maintaining a mischievous little grin, you may begin to notice the vibrations we make when we sing. When the engaged cheeks or smile is dropped, you will notice that the Buzz you feel in the front of your face disappears or moves back into your throat.

When our lifted cheek muscles are maintained, it's as if our sound is naturally directed to this Buzz spot, which will allow us to resonate more consistently and effectively. The challenge is that in many countries, our natural facial orientation tends to be dropped or very relaxed. When this occurs, our sound moves back into the mouth and throat, and feeling this Buzz becomes a challenge.

One other little way to feel this spot is to say AH like we normally would with our mouths and cheeks relaxed and then say it again with a mischievous little smile on our faces. You should immediately notice a difference in the quality of the sound. One will feel down and back and the other brighter and more in the front of our faces. Put one finger right under your nose and do it again. This time you may be able to feel the small vibration that moves as you change your mouth position. For me this little tiny Buzz holds one of the keys to the whole puzzle for us, especially those of us that are North American.

Just for the record, in a few instances the darker sound we naturally make when we are dropped can be seen as desirable in certain operatic or choral music where the director is trying to blend the sound of a large group of people. Rounded, dark vowels are considered somewhat easier to blend in the choral setting, especially if there is a mix of vocal abilities in the group. But the demands on the untrained singer become stressful, as these darker sounds are hard to support without assistance from the body. Once bel canto principles are established in the singer, this rounder sound is achieved with less constriction and more control, as we become the well-balanced instrument that resonates sound naturally.

If you have attended an opera at some point in your life, you may have found it difficult to understand what the singers were singing.

Sometimes this is due to the language barriers that exist when a work is performed in German or Italian and we are not fluent speakers of those languages. Other times, though, this lack of specific articulation is a by-product of the focus being mostly on this open, back vowel production, with very little emphasis on the consonants, so the words can tend to run together for the listener.

Today's current classical approach to singing, often does not work well for those that want to sing more contemporary styles of music. In addition to the focus on back production, there is too much air and power being put through the vocal mechanism. This is where the benefits of the bel canto approach become even more apparent.

If you have ever listened to a famous opera singer sing a pop song, you will know that there are times when they sound like opera-singers-singing-pop, versus the guy-or-girl-next-door-singing-pop. Once trained in opera, in most cases, it is very difficult to go backwards and sing without the open, big sound. Once the demands of composers like Puccini, Verdi, Bizet and Wagner hit the opera scene beginning in the mid-1800's, singers needed to find a way to produce a bigger, more powerful sound.

The bel canto orientation offers a unique opportunity for the singer who wants a more natural sound. It is a classical approach, but specific to a type of music that required a lighter production, allowing for the possibility of stylistic freedom today. This training allows us to go to the edge of the classical world, gleaning all of the good fundamental musculature and breath support information bel canto has to offer, without going over the fence and creating an over-produced, often heavily vibrato-oriented sound.

So, as we move forward in our discussion of bel canto and the Buzz, in addition to working on our breathing and musculature, we are going to talk about the difference between the way in which we say our vowel sounds, and the way the Italians produce theirs. The thing you will notice almost immediately as we do some practice in this awareness is that Italian vowels are in general brighter. This forward placement impacts our ability to sustain better intonation. When combined with the precise almost speech-like articulation of consonants, these pure, forward vowels will allow our diction to be more clearly understood, and the place where this all comes together is literally right under our noses, the secret spot called the Buzz!

The Core of the Voice Is Like the Center of a Carrot

Most of the students who come to me for training share one thing in common: voices that are out of alignment. So, we are going to talk for a minute about the principle of centering.

If you were to cut a carrot lengthwise down the middle, you would notice a slightly lighter line running up and down right in the center. For a minute, imagine that line as it relates to your voice.

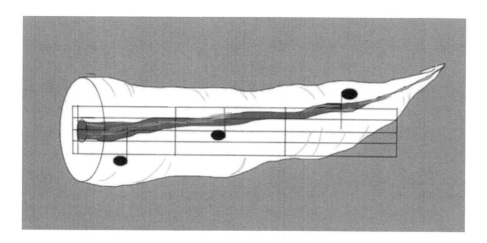

In order for us to bring your voice into alignment, we need to find the pathway that allows you to sing with ease from your very lowest note to your very highest, with the understanding that you have more notes available to you on both ends of your instrument than you have probably ever experienced.

If you imagine someone singing right on the absolute center of the pitch, not a little sharp and not a little flat, but right on the accurate tone—and continuing to do so on every note up and down their vocal range—this would represent the alignment of core sound in the person's voice.

Because of the nature of the Italian bright vowels I use, there may be a tendency for this work to feel more narrow and compressed when exercising. This is not only helpful, but it's also essential for bringing a singer into this vocal alignment. The higher we go in our range, when singing like this, the more we are likely to feel the vibration engage the bones of the face. When we get to a certain point, we may feel an intensity of pressure between the eyes. If unaccustomed to this feeling, we may want to back away from that sensation. This is what I mean when I talk about compression. Just know that, in time, you will become used to the experience and it will become less intense.

Singing is like any other athletic or spiritual practice, for in order for the sound to be beautiful, it will need to be lined up or brought into balance. In my experience, when this alignment happens, the voice will feel like it is riding up and down a little train track, and when that pathway is clear, well-marked and integrated into the body, it will make your singing effortless.

To understand the voice overall, we must first break it down into sections, or what voice teachers refer to as vocal registers. For women, there are three parts of the voice: the chest, middle and head registers. For men, those three exist with an additional section of the voice referred to as the *falsetto*.

In my bel canto training, I was taught to understand that there are certain parts of our vocal registers that feel more challenging, called the *passaggios*. An image that will help us understand this concept is the hourglass. In each register there are several notes that feel comfortable, which we manage to sing with great ease, but when we try to navigate through the transitions or passaggios themselves there can be an awkwardness articulating, sometimes quite suddenly, which is caused by this shift in registrations. The required brightening and lifting of the sound to maneuver through the transition can be equated to moving through the narrow neck of the hourglass.

These passageways are areas located between each register. When a singer gets to one of these spots, the voice will not feel like it wants to work in the same way, and in some cases the passaggio between the middle and head registers will stop singers completely, making them believe that they do not have the ability to sing high notes at all; this part of the voice is often referred to as the break by American voice teachers and coaches.

In some technical approaches, coaches use a two-part vocal template, incorporating the voice into only chest and head registers. This concept creates an even more obvious imbalance. Without acknowledging the middle register, the voice can often become too heavy as it drives up strong through the first half of the range, and then has to absolutely flip into an almost detached quality, referred to as the head voice. This two-part understanding almost certainly does cause a clear break to happen and it is often located outside of the natural passaggios. So for me, moving into a more comprehensive understanding of three registers for women, or four registers for men, allows for a more natural transitional process to occur for the singer, allowing us to eventually create one seamless voice from bottom to top.

So, as I talk about some of the principles that help us find our centered and well-balanced voice, we will address the pitfalls we may encounter and help you understand how to navigate through them. Even better, as time goes on, we will strengthen and integrate the transitions throughout the registers, so that ultimately you will no longer feel uncomfortable anywhere in your entire vocal range.

Sing Like a Romanian: The Benefits of Goofing Around

In the vocal studio, I will often use a variety of foreign accents in a humorous way in order to help a student relax and maybe even laugh a little. But, there is another method to my nutty ways! Sometimes in order to get our voices to work properly, we need to get the problems associated with the English language, especially Americanized-English, out of the way in order to feel something quite amazing and different.

Although it can feel silly or like it has no purpose, this goofing around helps the emotional body let go and our self-conscious natures to release. Just for a moment, try pretending that you are recreating a scene from Monty Python, or imagine that you are Julia Child or another famous foreign person, like Julie Andrews with her very precise enunciation. In the studio I often fall into a Romanian or other European accent when demonstrating this principle to my students.

This kind of playing around has a side benefit of preventing my mouth from opening too wide and helps keep my cheeks lifted or energized, engaging this place we call the Buzz. For example, overall when I goof around with a more Europeanized accent, the serious challenges the English language creates essentially disappear, allowing me to feel my voice differently. I will say when I am doing this, it feels like I don't speak English very well, which can feel a bit odd to us. If you will lift and sustain your cheek muscles while looking in the mirror, start to say a sentence and you may feel this affected sound I am talking about.

This kind of pretending can be very helpful down the road, when we are dealing with your specific vocal issues. Depending on where we are from, our unique vowel production, regionalisms and dialects—like the varied Southern accents and drawls, or the stereotypical New York or Boston accents—can affect our singing voices in a rather contraindicative way and finding creative ways for you to feel your voice differently becomes critical to the process of transformation.

Singing Is Kind of Like Flying an Helicopter!

At its very basic definition, singing is little more than the elongation of vowels. For example, if you say AH quickly and then repeat the AH again and hold it for just a couple more seconds, you will notice that the second sound now has a tone or pitch to it. It doesn't matter what that pitch is or whether you think it is in tune or not. Just notice that by sustaining the sound a tiny bit longer, you have created a tone. Take a moment to try it.

When I am describing the singing coordination process to someone really having difficulty, I remind them that the entire evolution is somewhat like the challenges associated with flying a helicopter, trying to encourage them to be patient with themselves and the process.

An airplane essentially revs up, gets lift, takes off and then once done flying, lands. A helicopter is a whole different experience. It can go up and down, side to side and back and forth. In essence, our voices have the same energetic counter-forces all working together within our bodies when we are sustaining good sound.

For example, when we get to our breathing process, we will find that our inhalation will be more effective when we think about filling the body with air horizontally. As our ribs and body expand this way, we will feel a stretch side-to-side, as opposed to downward.

Our second area of counter motion will occur as we energize the top jaw and area behind our eyes upward, while relaxing our tongue and jaw downward, at the same time. This contrary motion is what takes some time to wrap our thoughts around. We aren't accustomed to the oppositional energies we are feeling.

The third cross will occur with our articulation and breathing process, where the sound will be going forward, but we will feel ourselves controlling our breath, by holding back. As you can imagine, trying to keep all these elements engaged at one time might be a bit tricky. We will just take each piece of the puzzle step-by-step and start with the very essence of singing – elongated vowels.

As we extend the idea of elongated vowels to elongated speech, we will hit our first major challenge, since the primary problem we face as singers is our language itself and how we speak. This holds true for any language where the sounds or syllables close down or drop in inflection.

My first language is Americanized-English. If this is yours, no matter where you were raised there are some serious pitfalls that may be encountered while speaking, caused by diphthongs and certain consonants that directly impact our ability to sing with ease and beauty. The good news is that by understanding where the potholes are and how to maneuver around them, you will be able to remove these challenges and finally discover your own true voice.

Although some voice teachers may understand these language-based issues and share them with their private students, there is not widespread understanding about them in mainstream music education. When someone sings and sounds awful to us, we generally assume that person can't sing. And yet, with just a few muscular adjustments in our facial mannerisms, combined with this newfound awareness of the pitfalls, changes can be made that will almost immediately have a positive impact on the quality of the singing.

In fact, as we have said, the foundation of good singing really comes down to muscular activity in the mouth and body. These are elements that can be learned by anyone who has the desire to do so. Other aspects of singing that have to do with articulation, artistry and musicianship can also be learned. Certainly, some aspects of the process take longer to integrate than others. As we go along in the book, I will show you ways to ease the process along by making the steps enjoyable and adding humor to the process of self-discovery.

How An Italian Can Help Us Navigate This Course

So, have you ever watched an Italian person speak? What have you noticed about his or her energy and mannerisms that are distinctly different from the average American's? Often, they are more animated or more passionate in their speech, articulating their words very distinctly or precisely. Later on in the book, we will continue our discussion of how taking on a few of these mannerisms will help us sing.

It is an accepted fact that Italians are some of the best singers in the world (if not the best), and that Italian singing teachers are also considered superior. For years I wondered why that was the case, and what made them so very blessed to hold these esteemed positions. Well, when I finally found my last teacher and was introduced to the bel canto style of singing, I began to understand that this Italianate technique contained a secret spot that non-Italians could discover—the Buzz— that, when engaged, levels the playing field, so to speak, and assists us all to become better singers.

The following story illuminates this English closed-language problem, Italian language solution. A woman heard me sing at a Wayne Dyer presentation at the Maui Arts and Cultural Center, and was struck with the desire to ask me to coach her. It took her a few months to get up the courage to book a private session, but finally her desire to see if she could sing well outweighed her fear.

Mirka was a yoga instructor who loved to sing, but felt that she could only sing low notes and that the tone quality was not very good. She really wanted to be able to feel more comfortable, both with chanting in the yoga studio and singing for fun in her life, without feeling self-conscious.

I started at the beginning, talking about breathing, of which she already had some awareness with her Yoga practice, and basic breath support. As we began the warm-ups together and walked through the initial vocal exercises, I noticed that she was starting to feel uncomfortable.

So, I stopped the lesson and asked Mirka where she was from. I heard in her voice something that led me to believe that she was European. As it turned out, she was from Northern Italy. I asked her if she still spoke Italian fluently. She answered, "Yes." I shared with her that this was her lucky day, and that I wanted her to go back to her Italian roots and do the rest of the session as if she was once again speaking in her native language, utilizing her pure Italian vowels.

The first thing that happened was that she was able to do every one of my regular warm-up exercises without effort. Once Mirka reconnected with the sounds I asked her to use, she made the internal adjustment from English to Italian, as she shifted where she was focusing and feeling her vowels. This subtle adjustment caused each note she sang to be in perfect intonation, and she had no difficulty going from the low end to the high end of the scale within a standard healthy vocal range—in her case, about two octaves.

This ease of singing became even more apparent when I did something I normally never do. I asked her to sing the first Italian vocalise exercise from the *Vaccai*. This book contains a series of mini-songs written in 1830s by Nicola Vaccai and is considered rather standard repertoire within the Italian voice teaching community.

This is the point where I was stunned. First of all, here is a woman who has only been comfortable singing in her low register. Secondly, after being with me for about 30-minutes, she was about to sing straight through a rather challenging exercise that I normally don't even give a student until after two or three weeks of lessons.

Now remember, I believe that when all of our vowel sounds are made with a more forward or Italianate production, singing becomes easy. This student who came to me for assistance was about to validate that belief for me in an amazing way. What happened next I will never forget.

Mirka proceeded to sing the entire exercise that spans over an octave and a half, with absolute effortless quality, right on pitch with beautiful tone. Her natural singing voice came forth so quickly that it caught both of us off guard. She was in tears and I was smiling so big "I thought my face would crack," as my father used to say. Needless to say, she left the studio that day, knowing with certainty that she could sing and with some focused practice sing well.

Not too long after this visit from Mirka, another Italian young man came to me for assistance with his singing. He had lived in the United States for thirteen years and had only studied voice with American teachers. When he began vocalizing for me, it became obvious that his challenges were predominantly due to his newly learned Americanized vowel placement. When I asked him to go back to his Italian vowels and pronunciation, his voice also immediately shifted and became clear, strong and in tune, another demonstration of the power of these Italianate pure vowels, which we also overlaid and applied to his English songs that day.

These two people inspired my vision of bringing this awareness to singers who are struggling to create ease with their voices. My own life as a performer had been transformed from amateur to professional, just by shifting my vowel production from American speech-based chaos to magical Italian pure vowel placement ease. Your experience can be transformed, too!

So, let's start this journey to our well-balanced voices with the foundation of all good singing…breath support!

Chapter 2: How to Support Yourself

Lesson 1: As Boring As It Is...Breathing Is 75 Percent of the Game

The purpose of breath support is to provide the foundation for the voice, or vocal mechanism, so that all responsibility for making sound is taken off of the vocal cords and throat and put onto the body or torso. Good physical support facilitates effortless vocal production and will require a bit of coordination of muscles that we are not used to using in day-to-day activity.

This foundation of strength in the body becomes even more critical when someone is singing more intense styles of music, like blues and rock. In this day and age, when the songs many singers are singing are heavy and driving in nature, to not have the body take responsibility for the sound could cause a singer to lose his voice to fatigue or worse—vocal nodules. But even for the singer who is not singing a heavy or forceful repertoire, without good support there will be a tendency to lose control and feel strain as one is singing.

One of the conflicting concepts in the field of singing has to do with how the breath is utilized and maintained. There are two schools of thought – airflow vs. air pressure. In bel canto, support and breath control becomes a function of gentle, steady air pressure that is stimulated by a very small stream of air, regulated by the stabilized oscillation of the larynx without constriction and controlled by steady expanded ribs.

I am never trying to press or push air out of my body, but rather always trying to sustain an expanded ribcage. The maintaining of pressure is responsible for assisting me to handle lengthy phrases in a song and, perhaps more important, to help keep my vibrato even and stable. In the case of styles requiring what is called straight tone, as in

31

Gregorian Chanting and Barbershop, this sustainment of rib support that we are going to begin working on allows effortless maintenance of clear unwavering tone, without throat constriction.

Overall, the breath support mechanism involves the entire torso from the shoulders to hips, and if you are someone interested in singing opera, some would say all the way down to the feet. Keep in mind, those singers singing heavier operatic repertoire, like Puccini and Verdi, work for years to manage the power and size of breath they need to control. Contemporary singers do not face the same demands and therefore, do not need to manage the same quantity of air or power.

Nonetheless, the contemporary singer faces other challenges that tax the vocal mechanism. Hard, driving chest voice singing puts an enormous amount of pressure on the voice and tends to cause both constriction issues and vocal fatigue. In some cases, notes that are higher will seem to be completely out of reach. This is less a truism and more a result of lack of weight balance. There is a ratio of support to amount of power desired that must be sustained or the voice becomes taxed and liable to collapse.

Just know that when we are just learning to develop support and breath control, it is difficult to take a concept like support is the whole torso and do much with it, practically speaking. It is too broad an area to comprehend or integrate at one time. The abdominal muscles coordinate more naturally. But, the ribs will not engage if we aren't mindful of them. So, we are going to isolate our initial understanding in the ribcage area, the foundation of actual physical support.

In the beginning, as boring as it may seem—and it definitely was boring to me when I started doing the work—the breathing exercises included in this book are some of the most important exercises I can share with you. Not only will you be able to improve your overall sound by simply adding support, you'll also increase your ability to keep your voice healthy and well balanced. In truth, when your support engages, it often solves numerous problems, including smoothing out the vibrato and keeping the sustained tones steady.

One of the mistaken assumptions regarding breath support has to do with the diaphragm muscle. For years, voice teachers have taught students to sing from the diaphragm or use diaphragmatic support. The challenge that develops around this concept has to do with the diaphragm muscle itself. As I mentioned, the muscle itself is involved, but indirectly.

The diaphragm muscle's primary function is to separate the chest cavity from the abdominal cavity and, as an internal barrier muscle it goes across the body and prevents germs from the abdominal cavity from reaching the lungs and the heart. It is involved in the breathing process to the degree it becomes bowl-like to allow the lungs to drop lower into the abdominal area to fill up with air.

Many voice teachers speak to their students about using the diaphragm muscles to support their singing. A few years back, a study was done on the diaphragm as it related to singing, through the National Association of Teachers of Singing (NATS). This study was originally done to determine if we could even feel our diaphragm. The answer was no and, in my opinion, if you cannot feel a muscle it is virtually impossible to integrate it into the understanding of breath support. As this muscle is engaged by surrounding parts of the breath support mechanism, the ribs and abdominals, it becomes part of the process, but not something we can focus on controlling directly.

After studying with six teachers over a twenty-year period, I can honestly say the development of support was the most mystical process I had to endure along the way, until my work with my bel canto teacher. His clarity about how to exercise the musculature involved in actual support was part of the equation and his consistent, rather relentless communication of the importance of this piece of the singing puzzle was the motivation for continued practice and awareness on my part.

As a warning note, some teachers do not teach support at all. I cannot envision any circumstance in singing where this is not dangerous. For example, a few years back I got into a discussion with another voice teacher. I had been privy to hearing her lessons through the wall of a music conservatory at which I worked. I noticed something about her exercises that concerned me. She was using a series of intensely repetitive exercises that appeared to overwork the high or head register, exercises which I had been trained to avoid.

I approached her and asked about the technique she was using. To her credit, she was very open and gave me her technical manual to look at over a weekend. In reading this book, the first thing that popped out at me was that there was absolutely nothing in the manual about breath support. I decided to ask questions about why there was a lack of support in the technique. She said that there was a general concern that if a student learned breath support, they would then have too much power and would choose to over-blow air through the vocal folds and create problems for themselves.

There is a tiny bit of truth in what she was saying. Power can sometimes be misused, and over-blowing air can be problematic. However, not learning proper breath support or control of any kind could ultimately be disastrous for a singer, especially in hard driving contemporary music, where the risk of vocal strain and accompanying medical issues is a reality.

From the technical training point of view I come from, both the power and the control of the breath are addressed, so that a singer can have support and maintain a small enough quantity of airflow through the vocal folds to not only prevent any possibility of damage, but to also place the responsibility for making sound on the body, not the throat.

As I mentioned earlier, in some cases lack of breath support and control can directly contribute to the development of vocal nodules—areas on the vocal chords or folds that have been irritated by friction and become calluses. One can also develop polyps, which are more akin to blisters. The main difference is that nodules usually form more slowly over time than polyps.

These medical issues cause a gap to occur between the folds and when you go to sing you may hear an intense raspiness or breathy quality, like someone who has been a heavy smoker. Nodes can occur from general misuse, aggressive singing, smoking, smoking environments or even heavy coughing. Once nodules are developed they can be very difficult to get rid of without therapy or surgical procedures. These procedures are risky and although technology is improving, in many cases there is no guarantee that the folds will be able to coordinate for singing, once healed. Surgery should always be considered the last resort.

A good first step is to visit a qualified laryngologist or Ear, Nose and Throat (ENT) doctor, accustomed to working with singers. The doctor will look at your vocal cords and determine the cause of the problem and then make a referral for you to a speech pathologist. In any case, it will take time for the nodules or polyps to go away, but both may successfully be reduced or eliminated through therapy with a qualified pathologist who works with singers.

Sometimes putting intense pressure on the larynx over and over again for an extended period of time, for example eight shows a week, fatigues the instrument and when one's support is not solid, damage can occur.

It's a known fact that a Broadway belter will often have a very short stage career, unless they understand how to handle the demands on the voice. For example, the role of Fontine in *Les Miserables* is almost entirely belted. This essentially means that the weight of the lower register, the chest voice, is brought up all the way through the middle register and in this case, through the second passaggio. That power creates an amazing sound, but putting that kind of pressure on the voice can potentially limit your lifespan as a singer, unless you have been trained to support effectively.

My teacher was known for his work with recovering Broadway belters who had lost their ability to sing during the run of a show. Essentially, he would retrain their voices using the principles of bel canto, by pulling the voice all the way back in terms of pressure only allowing gentle vocalization, while establishing physical support in the body and realigning the vocal core. This work not only strengthened the singers, it often saved their careers and allowed them to return to Broadway.

Lesson 2: Ribs Do So Much More Than Hold Our Lungs in Place

So, let's address the ribcage. We'll integrate, slowly and methodically, a base of breathing support that will assist you in your singing process. Before we begin, we need to understand the nature of the muscles associated with the ribs.

The intercostal and extracostal muscles are the small muscles that line the inside and outside of the ribcage. They are involuntary muscles that for the most part haven't worked a day in their lives. As the lungs fill up with air, the ribs and the accompanying muscles are pushed out in the expansion. As the lungs release the air, the ribcage collapses. Because the rib muscles do not normally have to engage or work for natural breathing, they are not accustomed to staying energized. In order to do what we do, remember that we need to maintain a small, steady flow of air, while we maintain energized ribs that establish gentle, continuous air pressure.

Over the years, in working with singers who sing all sorts of music and repertoire, I have discerned that ultimately different amounts of support energy are required for the many different styles of music. The amount or percentage of support required for a pop, alternative or folk singer, for example, is dramatically different than the amount needed by an opera singer to sing a demanding aria. But, to experience our voices with clear tones and strong legato lines, all styles require an engaged, energized body.

Eight years ago, a beautiful young woman, Barbara, came to me for assistance. She sang R&B and rock music in her own band. Over a two-year period she had lost her voice innumerable times after playing gigs. It was starting to get to the point that she couldn't count on her voice to be there when she needed it and, having had to actually cancel a few gigs it was now impacting her pocketbook.

Barbara arranged her schedule to do some vocal work without putting any singing gigs on the calendar. We took the opportunity to take her back to ground zero and work on exercises that built her foundation of support, where previously there had been none.

If you watch a person sing who is not supporting herself adequately, you will notice that her throat is very busy and most of the time, intensely constricted. Muscles will appear to be tight and often look like they are popping out. The breathing exercise I am going to describe next is exactly the exercise I first used with Barbara, which ultimately helped save her career. After six months of working with me on all aspects of vocal production, she was able to go back out and sing the same repertoire and never again lost her voice due to strain.

Lesson 3: Floor-Work and Door-Work

If you will lie down on the floor on your back and put your hands over your abdomen, right near your belly button, we will begin.

- Exhale all the breath through the mouth.

- Inhale through the nose slowly.
- Repeat this 2-3 times.

You will notice that the abdominal muscles rise on the inhalation and lower on the exhalation. As air is drawn into the lungs, the abdominal muscles release or expand, allowing the diaphragm muscle to drop lower into the abdominal cavity. When the air is exhaled, the tummy pulls back in naturally and the air is essentially pushed out. This would be considered a natural breath, one that would occur when we are lying down or resting; it's the involuntary process we experience when we are walking around not paying much attention to our breathing.

I often say to my students that a singer's breath is not natural because it requires extra energy and intention. If we are to stabilize sound vibration, we need to establish a feeling of gentle air pressure by stabilizing our ribs in an open, energized way and limiting the amount of breath coming through the vocal cords to a small, steady stream. In order to do this, the ribs have to learn to stay still. You'll notice immediately after you inhale that they will pretty much want to collapse. Fighting that urge is the first step toward gaining control over this aspect of singing.

So, if you will draw your attention to the ribcage now, by placing your hands on the lower part of the ribs near the sternum, we will focus on developing rib strength.

- Exhale all the breath through the mouth.
- Inhale through the nose, expanding the ribcage.
- Exhale on a tiny "S" sound, like a baby hissing snake or leaking bicycle tire.

Once again, you should notice that the ribs expand during the inhalation and then as we exhale, the ribs want to slowly collapse.

If you will find a clock with a second-hand on it, you can time yourself. Just aim for 15-20 seconds at first and then eventually you will work your way up to 30-60 seconds sustaining your exhale. As an aside, men sometimes have longer initial times, as their chest cavities tend to be a bit larger and tend to have more natural chest strength.

Now we are going to work against that collapse and try to keep the ribcage lifted throughout the entire exhale.

- Exhale all the breath through the mouth.
- Inhale through the nose, expanding the ribcage.
- Exhale on a tiny "S" sound, keeping the ribcage lifted toward the ceiling.

Whether you are male or female, you will notice that the ribs will get tired and want to collapse before you are through exhaling all your air. This is completely normal, and as we mentioned previously the rib muscles lack strength at this point, unless you are an athlete that works this area of the body or a swimmer or runner who does a lot of cardio work. So we have to build up the strength of these muscles slowly.

I normally recommend that my students do this floor exercise every day for at least a couple of weeks to get started, and that two or three repetitions of the exercise is sufficient during any given practice session. This exercise can be done in the morning upon waking or in the evening as a way to unwind.

In order to jump start rib strength, especially for students who are not big into exercise or are over 40, I will also occasionally suggest doing "isometric" rib exercises. This is a stationary exercise designed only to work the ribs, not focusing on the breath aspect at all. Isometrics entail tightening a muscle area, holding for a short period of time and then releasing the tension.

To work the ribs in this fashion, I breathe into the ribs, and then hold the rib muscles out horizontally, as if I am filling up a tin can. Then, not allowing the sides of the can to collapse, I keep the ribcage open. Imagine that you are filling up a container with air and then working to maintain the filled container, without letting any air go.

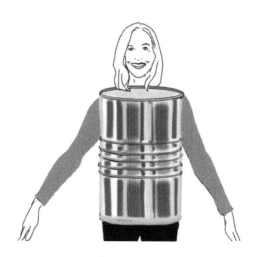

Maintain this expanded position for a count of 6 and then release. It will feel like you are holding your breath for a few seconds on this exercise. In truth, we won't ever really be holding our breath while we sing, but for purposes of just getting the ribs oriented to work harder, this isometric process can be helpful. Three repetitions of this exercise are sufficient for each session. By incorporating this exercise, I have found that students with little or no upper body strength develop some core strength fairly quickly.

Another way to feel the engagement of the rib muscles is to assume the "Diva" stance. Do you ever remember seeing pictures of old time operatic sopranos standing with their hands clutched in front of them, sort of under their bosoms? Do you know what they were doing? We generally think they were just standing their looking poised, but in fact they were assisting themselves in maintaining support.

If you will assume that position, keeping shoulders down, grasp your hands right in front of the sternum with arms parallel to the body, and pull your hands in opposition, you will notice that the lateral and rib muscles become engaged or energized in your back at the sides of the ribcage. It is a very small movement, about a quarter to half of an inch additional expansion from your inhale position. If you feel the shoulders rising while doing this exercise, start over, making sure that your inhalation is only into the lower part or base of your ribs. You can also push your hands against each other in this same position and find another way to feel those same side muscles as well, although I find that pulling gives more of a sense of expansion and pushing them together, more of a tightened feeling.

Until the body has integrated the muscle memory of what it means to engage, energize and support the sound, even if this Diva position looks a little silly, it can be very helpful in identifying where and how the rib engagement actually occurs.

Another way you can get assistance with your rib strength development is to get a friend, partner, or spouse to help you. Asking them to stand behind you, have them place their hands on the lower back and sides of your ribs. You then want to inhale through your nose, expanding your lower ribcage area laterally or horizontally, right where their hands are situated. You then will ask them to press gently but firmly on your ribs, while you resist their pressure, by pressing your ribs outward towards their hands. Now exhale on the tiny "S." Initially, you will find the breath harder to control under these conditions. The benefit is that this practice will give you a little more resistance while helping you develop additional rib strength, once you have achieved a baseline comfort with the previous exercises.

If you've ever taken a dance class, you may remember that the body posture required standing up straight, with shoulders down and back, chest up and derriere tucked slightly. This is the same posture I use while practicing singing. It helps keeps the whole mechanism in alignment while we focus on our vocalizing. Oh, yes, and remember to keep your knees a little bit bent.

I have yet to have anyone faint on me; however, there have been moments where students have felt light-headed and needed to sit for a moment. Breathing like this oxygenates the body a bit more than normal breathing, and sometimes it takes a little getting used to. Remember that we want to inhale slowly, almost without sound, so that the airflow over the vocal cords is gentle and almost imperceptible. Once standing and doing this exercise feels comfortable, we are going to take it to a wall or a door.

Remember in high school P.E. class where you had to do standing push-ups up against a wall or door? Essentially you are putting your hands on the wall, shoulder-width apart and standing about a foot or so from the wall. If you lean in slightly bending the arms, you should feel a stretch occur along your lateral muscles. These are the muscles along the sides of your ribcage, towards your back. As you lean into the wall, you should be able to engage those muscles and create a bit of tension.

Now, in my mind, there is good tension and bad tension. If it is tension in the throat, I normally consider that bad. If we sustain gentle expanded tension in the torso, or body, that can be quite productive. We are going to use this push-up position on the wall or a door and try the breathing exercise again.

- Exhale all the breath through the mouth.
- Inhale through the nose, bringing the attention to the side muscles of the ribcage.
- As you lean into the wall, exhale slowly on a tiny "S" sound.
- Assume a neutral position and repeat the exercise 2 more times.

This wall exercise is another way to strengthen the sides of the ribs. The stronger these muscle are, the less effort it will take on your part to create a sense of energy or engagement in your body. If you already work out regularly lifting weights or swim, you may find you are able to do these exercises with less difficulty.

In all variations of the breathing exercise we are accomplishing several things. We are strengthening the actual muscles that help anchor the support, extending our ability to control our breath, and teaching the vocal mechanism itself how little air flow through the vocal cords is required to make sound. We are literally training our internal musculature to integrate and regulate the breath control process, just by doing the exercises.

There is one final breathing exercise that you can utilize to begin to incorporate the abdominals into the action. In my experience, when I am singing a difficult aria or song, I notice that my abdominals, legs and derriere engage to assist my support function through the piece. So it is important to understand how the abdominal muscles naturally move during an exhalation. For me, these muscles integrate naturally and do not require me to push them out or pull them in, in general. For if I do, I run the risk of blowing too much air through the vocal folds. However, in the case of very high notes, the abdominals can help increase the air pressure through additional momentum by pulling in slightly. This is a more advanced technical process and will be addressed later in the book.

- If you can bend over like a rag doll, do so now with head and arms hanging down toward floor.

- Exhale all your breath through the mouth.
- Inhale through the nose.
- Then exhale on a SH sound while you roll up the spine.

- As you get to the top, extend your ribcage and allow your shoulders to roll into position for proper posture.

- Repeat the entire exercise one more time.

This exercise gently shows the natural upward rolling movement that occurs in the abdominals on the exhalation, while supporting with the ribcage. From my experience, all of these muscle groups eventually integrate into one fluid motion. However, it does take some focused practice. As I mentioned previously, I would recommend doing three repetitions of any one of these breathing exercises every day. If you will do so, you will find that within a couple of weeks to a month you will have a very different experience of your body's strength and its ability to handle longer singing phrases.

Support is the most challenging issue to resolve for all of us as singers. Singing takes more energy, mentally and physically, than we may want it to and sometimes that stops some of us. But, even though this is kind of like going to the gym for the voice, I highly recommend sticking with it. There is a point that you will come to when the breathing just starts working naturally, without you having to over-think the process, but it definitely takes a few months for that to occur. So please be patient with the breathing and do your exercises. It will pay off!

Once you have isolated and exercised the ribs and lateral expansion of the support mechanism, adding a pelvic floor lift, or Kegel, will help stabilize and gently regulate your air flow.

Now this little anecdote illustrates the importance of support and how it can reverse and correct vocal challenges. A few years back an 80-year-old woman, Mary, approached me about her singing. She had sung soprano most of her life in her church choir. She timidly admitted that although she still loved to sing, her ability to do so was seriously affected by her age. Mary bravely shared with me some of her personal experiences and the issues she noticed as being particularly challenging. She said that her ability to breathe and control her vibrato was being severely hampered by her lack of energy.

At that time, she asked if I thought there was anything she could do. Smiling, I replied, "Yes."

Mary had developed what we call affectionately a wobble. This is what happens to the group I call—Sopranos Without Support. Most women over the age of 40 actually suffer from major support issues, unless they have been trained to avoid them, because our bodies change so dramatically through middle age. However, I have seen student after student shift that dilemma by doing some serious and diligent support work.

I carefully got this gal down on the floor and walked her through the basic breathing exercise. I showed her how to monitor her ribcage and how to limit the amount of airflow through the vocal cords. Mary agreed to do an intensive class with several other students, committing to a six-week process and also committing to continue her work at home. A few weeks later, she came into class beaming after being at church. She exclaimed, "I can sing again!"

In my opinion, it is never too late to improve one's ability to sing with more ease, no matter how old you are.

Lesson 4: Bow-and-Arrow Approach To Breath Preparation

When I am preparing to sing a phrase, I think about something I call the Bow-and-Arrow approach.

As I inhale, I feel the intake of air into my mouth, as if I am pulling back on a bow. If you have ever held a bow and arrow, you will remember that there is a feeling of stretch backwards that has to go all the way to the extreme position before the arrow can be released properly.

You may also remember that if you lift your head and you pull back on the bow, the arrow will fly right up into the air. But, if you cock your head down about a half an inch, as you aim toward your target, you can hit the center of the bull's-eye. In preparing to articulate sound, this image of fully preparing the stretch in the back of our mouths can be very helpful. Often our challenges with articulating occur because the muscles at the back of the throat are not quite in proper position.

So, if you exhale, think of an AH in your mind, and inhale slowly with your mouth open, you should start to feel a stretch occur in the back of your throat. Exhale again. Now repeat the process. Think AH and inhale very slowly noticing that stretch, taking it as far back as you can. There will come a point where you know you can't pull back anymore.

This stretch is the beginning of what I call the breath prep. It helps put the musculature into the best possible position for articulation. As we go forward with our lessons, we will refer to this breath preparation as we integrate other principles of good vocal production.

Chapter 3: Say AH

Lesson 5: Notice the Vibe

Let's talk about the essence of sound itself: vibration.

I would like you to take your two index fingers and place them alongside the jawbone, right in front of your ears, one on either side of your face. Three-quarters of each finger should be pressed up against the jaw.

Say OO firmly and extend it for 4 or 5 seconds.

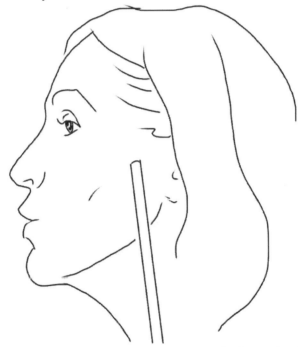

What did you feel? If you're not sure, do it again. You should notice a vibration of sound that is located at the back of the mouth or throat.

Now, I want you to move your fingers forward on your face about an inch and a half, keeping the fingers connected to the jawbone.

Say O firmly and extend it for 4 or 5 seconds.

What did you notice? Correct: vibration. Now, we are going to continue moving forward along the jaw another inch or so and this time:

Say AH firmly and extend it for 4 or 5 seconds.

Again, you will feel vibration, although in my experience the AH is the hardest to feel. Now, once again move the fingers forward to your smile lines.

Say A firmly and extend it for 4 or 5 seconds.

You should feel a vibration right in your smile lines. Finally, place your index finger right in front of your lips, keeping the finger touching the skin.

Say E firmly and extend it for 4 or 5 seconds.

Here you will feel what I call forward vibration, right in the front of your face.

The purpose of this exercise is to bring your awareness to the mouth and where you naturally resonate or vibrate the Americanized-English vowel sounds. You will notice that each of the sounds vibrates in a predominant position in the mouth, moving from back to front. The OO sound is the farthest back and the E vowel is the most forward, or brightest sound we make.

Often, as I mentioned briefly earlier, when a new student comes to the studio, we will start with the very essence of singing and sound, and how to notice where we are actually feeling our voices vibrate. Believe it or not, learning to feel your voice in your body instead of trying to listen to yourself inside your head helps you to sing with more ease. In those times when it is difficult to hear yourself in a chorus or other acoustically awkward environment, feeling your voice resonate properly is priceless.

Now take a moment and just hum one note, somewhat in the lower end of your range. The tone or pitch you choose to sing is almost irrelevant at this point. I usually don't recommend doing this on a high note, because it can get tiring.

What do you notice? You should feel a vibration, most likely at this point in the exercise it will occur in your throat. If you repeat the hum one more time and put your hand on your throat, you will be able to feel the vibration directly.

Now, I would like you to do it again. This time I want you to smile a little mischievous smile and hum the same pitch again, by articulating a clear M. Be sure that your lips are firmly placed together, and make the hum a little bit louder. You will notice that the vibration moving up to the front of the face may still be felt somewhat in the throat, but if you put your finger in front of your lips, you should be able to feel a small vibration there, as well.

The art of singing, at its most basic level, is about feeling the vibrations we create and directing those to specific areas of our mouth in order to maximize our effectiveness at resonating. Now this sounds pretty sexy, but the reality is that it is like a game of hide n' seek. Sometimes the voice will appear to be hidden or muffled or swallowed, but when energetically redirected, the voice will, all of a sudden, make an appearance that feels rather amazing. I have seen, time and time again, this one particular pleased look on my friends' and students' faces as they discovered their ability to sustain good pitch, and make sound that is beautiful.

The woman responsible for me finally writing about this ease of singing was an example of this. I was preparing for a large meeting with a group of women friends. As the evening progressed, Jane and I began chatting about how she had written several children's songs, but couldn't sing them. I asked her why she felt that way and Jane shared her story with me about her early life and negative feedback she had received as a child. After giving her my opinion that what had happened to her was wrong and nothing more than hurtful, I asked her if she would try something.

Jane agreed and was very good-natured about playing a song on the piano that she had written. At this point she did not sing the words, she just played the accompaniment music. I asked her to give me the words to just the first sentence of the song, which she did. Then I asked her to try and sing it. Clearly the notes and words felt awkward and somewhat jumbled in her mouth.

So I asked her if she would be willing to try something and again she said, "Yes" wholeheartedly. I had her stand up straight and smile. I asked her to open her mouth just a little bit and say AH. She did. While sustaining the smile, I asked her to say the AH again, this time holding it a few seconds longer. The look on her face when she made that sound was priceless: for in that simple moment of just lifting into a small smile and saying a nice long AH, she made her first lovely singing sound.

At that point, I had Jane prep herself the same way—breathe into that back-of-the-throat stretch and then try to maintain that smiling lift—while singing the first line of her song. She did so and was tickled with her results. It was the first time she had ever felt herself sing something she wrote, and she actually liked what she heard.

I have found over the years that it is the smallest breakthroughs that create the biggest growth, even for myself, and these little things have often carried the greatest impact. In our society where everything is based on instant gratification, this can be both good and bad news for the ability to notice the small details sometimes gets buried under loads and loads of expectation and frustration.

Singing well has lots of little details to it. But, by building understanding step-by-step, we are able to retrain the mind to think properly and focus its attention on those pieces of the puzzle that will put the musculature into proper position to sustain good sound. Taking this process slowly allows for a full integration of all components which, once felt, will start to make sense to the mind and become automatic practice.

Lesson 6: Feel Your Vowels...No, Really *Feel* Your Vowels

In Lesson 5 we felt our vowels vibrate in our mouths from back to front— from OO to E. However, if we had been born in Italy, we would have learned to feel our vowels in a distinctly different way.

So, once again, bring your index finger up to your lips, with the bottom of your finger connected to the jaw, then smile and say quickly and firmly in consecutive order, with Italian equivalent in parentheses: E (i), A (e), AH (a), O (o), U (u=oo).

If you keep that little smile on your face while saying all of these sounds, you will notice that the vibration remains intact in the front of your face. If you drop the smile, the vibration will move back into a deeper part of your mouth. This one little realization was the beginning of a major shift in my own vocal technique. Italians literally feel their vowels in a frontal position in their mouths, whereas Americans unconsciously resonate vowel sounds throughout the mouth cavity.

This movement of sound is one of the reasons why singers in the U.S.A. often sound like they are chewing their words. For example, if you exaggerate your speech and slow down your words, you may be able to notice how this happens even in your own speech. There is sort of an up-and-down feeling that occurs as we say a sentence. You may even notice a natural pitch change from syllable to syllable or word to word. This up-and-down, in-and-out motion of sound is what causes us to appear to be out of tune. We may even be singing the right pitch, but it will often sound flat, just because it is hanging out too far back in our throat.

So what do we do if our language's vowel orientation, regionalisms and dialects are the direct cause of the problems we encounter when we sing? Together we are going to explore the nature of these language issues to see if we can integrate a few principles that will help make our singing effortless.

Lesson 7: Disturbing Diphthongs

The simplest definition of a pure vowel is the absence of the diphthong. The *Oxford English Dictionary* defines a diphthong as a "sound formed by the combination of two vowels in a single syllable."

In English our diphthongs are A, I and O and if you will take a moment to say these letters very slowly, you will feel how each vowel sound has two parts, with the second part dropping the pitch or tone. What is interesting to me however, as an American, is that we tend to apply this two-part sound to all of our vowels, even if they aren't actually diphthongs. It is as if our diphthong usage sets us up to close even our E, forcing us to drop the pitch as we finish the sound. You can imagine that if we drop the back half of every single syllable we sing, how difficult it might become to sustain good intonation.

Now there are only two pure vowel languages in the world…one of them is Italian and the other is Hawaiian. An interesting singing fact emerges from this language connection. As I mentioned earlier, when the Hawaiian language was put into written form, they used the Italian/Latin language as the basis for translation.

Having lived in the Hawaiian Islands for more than half of my life, I grew to know the local culture and its music, and what I discerned is that most Hawaiians have the potential to be natural singers, as do their Italian counterparts. Not only does Hawaii have an environment that supports its people singing for joy in general, but they also have this pure vowel language that makes it easy to sing. Most Hawaiian singers—whose first language is Hawaiian—are not found in a vocal studio studying how to be singers; most of them can just do it with ease, because their vowels naturally resonate in the forward position.

A challenge we face (often without knowing it) is that, as we maneuver up and down our vocal range or registers, each individual vowel changes depending on whether we are low or high. This problem is compounded by our body, which gets fearful when something feels like it is about to get difficult or too high or too low in our range and believe it or not, automatically does everything backwards. Singing is counter-intuitive to a great degree. This collision of body and vowel will impact our ability to hold steady on our pitch.

The power of pure vowels is going to be one of the greatest lessons we can learn as singers for, once stabilized forward, the vowels do not change quality as we sing, no matter where we are in our range. Because of the ease this creates for us, this one piece of the puzzle helps to alleviate the body's fear and allow for proper resonation. When this happens, it is much easier to stay in tune and create beautiful sound. Let me share with you my story about this particular point.

Back in the shower-practicing days in San Francisco, I kept up this curious practice of focusing on only the vowel sounds and keeping them bright, forward and consistent, so that every AH was exactly the same Italian AH and every E was exactly the same E and so on...every time I sang the sound.

One day after an extended time practicing this way on the first Vaccai exercise, *la scala*, I was able to focus on feeling every vowel staying in exactly the same forward position or spot, right under my nose—the place I call the Buzz. This was the day I had my absolute biggest breakthrough, in all the years I studied voice.

When every vowel sound was produced in exactly the same way, in the same forward position, singing suddenly became effortless. It was as if I had been singing with ease my entire life. I knew in that moment that singing for me had been utterly transformed. I did not need to be Italian or Hawaiian to experience this ease. Finally, I understood something that these cultures felt naturally, and of which they were most likely completely unaware.

One of the differences between their languages and those of us that speak with closed vowel sounds, is Italian and Hawaiian create what we would feel as a sort of unfinished quality to each syllable. Where our diphthong causes us to create two parts to our vowels, they only have essentially the first half. I needed to get used to that rather odd feeling this approach created, as nothing ever dropped or closed the way it did in my natural speech habits. The diphthong still gets turned and finished, but not until the absolute last second. Believe it or not, a side benefit to this kind of vocal production is clearer diction. This sustainment of what barbershoppers call the target vowel, or primary vowel sound, makes it easier for your audience to also understand the words by not finishing the diphthong too soon. We also then avoid the vowel collapse that normally distorts the intonation, which for barbershoppers in particular, then stabilizes what they call the lock and ring, the sustainment of the fifth note in a four-part harmonic chord.

In my moment of awareness that day, the transformation was extraordinary. High notes no longer felt high, low notes no longer felt heavy and weighty, the phrases I was singing became melodious and lyrical and once I had had that experience, I was free. I knew that there would be nothing I couldn't sing—from Broadway to pop, standards to folk music. It was the moment I took a quantum leap from amateur to professional, for once I understood how to control my sound and keep it stable and well-tuned, I never lost that ability and the practice of consistency was right around the corner.

Next we'll be talking about the vocal mechanism, or musculature, in simple terms and how watching what the professionals do can help you to find your own voice.

Chapter 4: Things That Are Liable To Make You Crazy

Lesson 8: That Darn Tongue and Jaw!

As we move forward to understanding our voices and how they work, we must address some of the predominant muscles and bones in the mouth. I like to refer to my two most favorite as that—darn tongue and jaw duo. As I often say to my students, most singers have either tongue or jaw tension to deal with.

Very few people coming into my studio are stress-free. Unfortunately, it appears to be the nature of our times for stress to be so present in our day-to-day lives. It is no wonder that we hold tension in areas of our body that are connected to releasing the voice. Just think of your communications lately and I'll bet that you can find a stressful situation somewhere around you—either at home or at work. So, when it comes to singing, some of that stress automatically carries over into our musculature.

Just for fun, let's start with the tongue. Most people don't realize that the tongue is a very large muscle, which connects way down at the base of the throat. The tongue is strong and sometimes contributes to our vocal challenges. As I understand it, this muscle has the capacity to put 6-10 pounds of pressure on the back of our front teeth, almost constantly. As a child I had to do tongue retraining exercises to keep me from having to get braces. I was beginning to develop an overbite and by doing tongue therapy, where I was taught how to swallow properly, my parents were able to avoid having to take me to the orthodontist.

Because this is an involuntary muscle and it has been moving around in your mouth your whole life without your conscious awareness, there is a reason that heeding the old adage "control your tongue" can be so difficult. It is not just a comment about appropriate behavior in our communication. Controlling one's tongue, when it comes to singing, can be quite a humorous exercise.

One of the things we are going to discuss in a later chapter is how looking in the mirror at our own mouths, watching what we are doing, will assist us to change all sorts of habits and behaviors. In the meantime, watch what other people do when they sing. There are many great singers in the world who are on television or YouTube.com, whom we can watch without having the scrutiny put on us. For example, if you like classical music, opera singers like Kiri Te Kanawa or Bryn Terfel or even the group *Il Divo* demonstrate good mouth position. Pop singers like Barbara Streisand, Mariah Carey, Celine Dion and in the Italian world, *Il Volo*, all exhibit the different aspects of good vocal production.

If you watch their mouths while they are sustaining a longer note, you will most likely notice that their mouths are rather cavernous! Their tongues are down and the roof of their mouths is lifted and high, so that a nice round space exists in their mouths. We talk about the roof of the mouth later on, so for now we'll stay with our discussion of the tongue.

If you are curious, here's an exercise to demonstrate how your tongue behaves in your own mouth. Go to a mirror right now and open your mouth wide. I want you to try and make your tongue lay flat on the bottom of your mouth, with a concave curve in it—a little scoop or u-shape on the floor of the mouth, by your lower teeth.

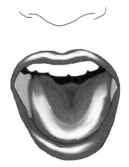

If you are really lucky, it will go into this position with little or no effort. However, normally the tongue doesn't like to cooperate so easily. Sometimes it will pull back and block the back of the throat by the uvula and sometimes it will sort of squeeze together into a narrower shape, getting kind of hard. By now you may have noticed that it doesn't like behaving the way we want it to and when you tell it what to do, it will very likely do something quite the opposite!

No matter how the tongue wants to behave initially, our goal is to train it to lay flatter, along the bottom of the mouth. It may take some time to retrain the muscle and we do that by gentle repetitive behaviors. Being patient at this stage is a very good idea. Remember that little steps ultimately create big results!

I refer to these next steps as a form of cellular muscle memory retraining. Once reoriented and exercised patiently, the tongue will no longer cause you the problems you may be dealing with now, such as tightness or constricted sound made when it covers up the opening at the back of the throat. So, there are a couple of exercises that can assist us to take back control.

One exercise involves looking in the mirror, placing the tongue on the floor of the mouth, letting it sink down in a U shape and saying AH. If the tongue comes up when you say the sound, stop and try again. The goal is to get the tongue to stay still on the bottom of the mouth in this concave shape, while saying the vowel sound. To help get the AH placement in a more forward or Italianate position, give yourself permission to make a mischievous little smile while doing this exercise.

It will feel awkward at first to be opening your mouth to get your tongue down flat and then asking yourself to smile a bit at the same time. This is just the first time you are encountering what I call a vocal duality or opposition of musculature. We are going to be starting to get used to lifting and lowering at the same time. Initially, this may feel challenging or even for some a bit impossible, but stick with it. Just take it slow.

Start with opening your mouth gently, not too wide, but wide enough to see your tongue. Now, while maintaining that position, lift your upper lip enough to see your top teeth. It will feel a bit like you are baring your teeth or creating a fake smile. The mouth will feel awkward in this position.

Now, let's try the exercise again. Make the tongue super soft, like you are going to talk sort of silly. Relax the tongue on the bottom of the mouth, like it is sinking down on the bottom between your teeth.

You can do this by inhaling as you lower it into place. If the tongue starts to pull back into the throat, attach the tip of the tongue onto your front bottom teeth, as if there is an imaginary piece of Velcro there. Now lay the tongue down and breathe in again, thinking AH. You have just prepped the mouth for articulation. Say AH, keeping the tongue in the down position.

If you were able to do this successfully, then breathe and do it again 2 or 3 more times. If the tongue was not cooperative, then just focus your attention on getting the tongue down on the floor of your mouth. Even this may take some coaxing and you may find that your tongue is so busy on its own that you can't seem to get control of it at all. Not to worry, this is normal. Just stop, take a deep breath and try again.

An advanced version of this exercise is to go through these five basic vowel sounds: AH, A, E, O and U (OO).

The tongue starts in the neutral, low position in the mouth for the AH and then maintaining that flattened, concave shape, we will slide the tongue forward, so that the tip of the tongue is just slightly extended over the bottom lip and say, A.

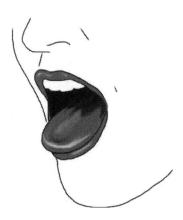

Once achieved, we will then slide the tongue out of the mouth another inch or so, while we say, E.

Then, slide the concave tongue back into the mouth to the initial position to say both the O and the OO sounds. The vowels you are able to articulate in this exercise will sound thick and dull. Not to worry too much about this, as our primary objective is to keep the tongue down.

Practicing this exercise slowly and gently is a necessity, for if we rush the tongue in and out of the mouth, without achieving the proper position, we are essentially training it to get in the way again. Muscles are funny that way. If we focus on training them to behave the way we want to, we will get control of them in time. If we go unconscious while attempting this work, then they will continue to cause us issues.

This muscle is one of the most difficult to get to behave, mainly because it has been doing its own thing for your whole life without you being aware of it. Trying to reclaim control over the tongue can sometimes feel like a major feat, but with gentle, repetitive practice, you will find that it will start to do what you want it to do and, more importantly as a singer, when you want it to do it!

Another exercise that is particularly helpful is called a tongue trill. If you remember being asked to roll your R's for Spanish or Italian class, it is done in a similar fashion, like a purring sound. (As an aside, there are some people who have difficulty rolling their R's. If you are one of these folks, just skip this exercise, as it is for relaxation more than training.)

If you can roll your R's, then do so on a somewhat lower pitch or tone. Then you are going to do what I call pitch circles. Begin on a low tone, it doesn't matter which one, then in one smooth movement, trill up to a higher pitch, sliding through all the in-between tones, and then return to the original lower tone; keeping the rolling sound going during the whole pitch circle and doing this on one breath. Each time you repeat the exercise you can go a bit higher in the circle of tones, with the goal to make it back down to the original pitch or tone in one breath.

When you are first trying to get your tongue to behave itself, I recommend doing both of these exercises for two to three weeks, doing three to four repetitions of each. One way to remember to do your tongue work is to tape a note on your bathroom mirror and do the exercises when you brush your teeth. Once a day is fine, but frankly the more frequently you do them, the sooner you will get the results, so twice a day won't hurt.

When I was practicing these exercises in the beginning, I noticed an amazing difference in how my tongue behaved after a couple of weeks. All of a sudden I could keep my tongue position low in my mouth without having to fight the muscle, while I was singing. This relieved me of the constriction and tightness I had previously felt in the sounds I was making. As a side note, often, I will continue to keep the tip of the tongue connected to the back of my lower front teeth as if I have a little piece of Velcro connecting it there. This is sort like giving the tongue a home base, only using it for articulation purposes and then sending it right back where it belongs—down and out of the way. Maintaining the lower tongue placement has a secondary benefit, too. It helps keep the larynx or vocal folds lower in the throat, a desirable position for singing.

So let's move on to another culprit in vocal tension—the jaw. So what about the jaw and how do we know if we are dealing with jaw tension? The other day I was working with my student Teri. As she turned sideways while warming up, I noticed a behavior I had not seen before. She was jutting her jaw forward on every single cut-off or end of phrase. In other words, when she went to end a note, Teri would stick out her jaw and kind of grab or bite at it to get the sound to stop.

I stopped her and asked her to notice was happening. She was completely unaware of that particular behavior, so I asked her to stand really still, look in the mirror and try to end or release the sound without making it happen with her jaw, just by focusing on releasing the sound with her mind. It took a little time to get used to that feeling and she was pleasantly surprised at the more effortless result.

Another student had a difficult time opening his mouth at all. He could open maybe a half an inch or so, but when I ask him to open his mouth any wider it was very hard for him to do so. Tom has a stressful job and is working on singing as a hobby, so I have been working with him to feel his jaw differently, without adding additional stress to his life.

Muscle tension takes a little time to shift, but with patience and diligent attention, the various stresses that show up in the tongue and jaw can be relieved. One exercise I often recommend to my students is something anyone can do when they are relaxing or watching television. Take your jaw in your hands, like you are cupping it from below and allow the jaw to relax into your hands, holding it firmly yet gently. You can then do a soft chewing motion up and down and then gently allowing it to move from side to side.

While you are working with your jaw, if you will make your tongue soft, like you are going to talk in that silly sort of relaxed voice, you can get the whole mechanism—jaw and tongue——to have a mini-relaxation massage. For folks who experience a lot of tension in either the jaw or tongue, giving the face a break by supporting it with the hands and giving it a little time to just move without constriction can be very helpful. Eventually this will allow the muscles to take on the new behaviors of lying down and opening or releasing more easily, in order to begin creating more resonance space inside the mouth.

In singing there are two ways to open the jaw. One is by hinging and opening the mouth really wide. The problem with this orientation, you will notice, is that it seems to decrease the amount of space in the back of mouth. This will be contrary to what needs to happen eventually—a more lifted, energized soft palate.

The second way to open the jaw is by dropping the back of the jaw down slightly separating the molars and gently easing it backward slightly toward the throat. This actually creates more space in the back of the mouth and offers us a win-win situation when we go to resonate sound effectively with a more lifted soft palate.

One way to create this same sensation is by placing our fingertips on each side of our face, between our upper and lower molars, and slightly pressing in, gently creating space between the teeth, by moving them apart.

If you try talking while keeping the teeth separated like this, you may feel like you are talking like Jimmy Stewart or the guy from Family Guy, who doesn't articulate very well and, of course, if you are having trouble, do the above backwards. Talk like Jimmy Stewart or that guy and your teeth will automatically separate. This more relaxed lower jaw position is very helpful for singing through the difficult parts of the voice, like the passaggios, and especially the highest notes we sing. Again, the open space created by a lifted energized upper jaw and palate combined with a relaxed lower jaw and tongue creates more resonance room and allows sound to spin or vibrate without constriction. This is a counter motion, however, and takes time to get used to. When I say lift and relax at the same time, most students go through a period of confusion, where they can only do one or the other. In time, the oppositional energy of being lifted and lowered will feel normal and you will be able to engage your inner amphitheater with ease.

As a side note, for barbershoppers this combined up and down position is what will create the tall sound so often described in various coaching sessions. The issue of being wide or bright goes away by creating a stable, round instrument within the mouth.

Lesson 9: The P Word: *Passaggios* and What To Do About Them

Now let's talk about an area of singing that impacts every person trying to do it— men and women, boys and girls. When you listen to someone sing, sometimes you will hear different qualities of sound as they sing low notes and high notes. It is common for the voice to be very strong on the low end and appear to weaken as it goes higher. But occasionally the opposite will be true—a light soprano may not be able to sing low notes at all, but can sing with ease on the top part of her range. Both of these situations indicate a voice that is not centered and lined up. Oftentimes, this lack of vocal alignment is caused by the transitions in our voices not being recognized and addressed. Understanding the nature of the voice can help us as well align our instruments, so that we have full access to our vocal range.

In our American system of vocal training, you may have heard someone use the term—break—along the way. Sometimes a singer will say, "Oh, I can't sing that note very well, because it is in my break." Well, I'll never forget the first time I used that word with my bel canto teacher. It happened only once!

He informed me that there was no such thing as a break, and that using that word in reference to our voices implied that something was broken, causing more problems for the singer. In my experience with these areas of the voice, I have come to deeply agree with him. Our minds are very powerful, and if we think there is a problem, we will manifest one!

This is another example of how the Italians have great information about the nature of our voices. Instead of breaks, I like to affectionately refer to these areas as the P word—for passaggio in Italian. My younger students refer jokingly to their pistachios when we are working with them in the studio.

Passaggios, which means passageways, refer to the transitional areas of the voice. These places in the vocal range feel odd and at times even un-sing-able. They occur on slightly different notes for heavier or lighter voices, but are all within a standard range. Usually a heavier voice will experience the passaggios starting two-to-three notes earlier than the lighter voice.

One way I have described the experience of going through a passaggio is like this: imagine an hourglass image—at the base of the hourglass, or while singing in the actual chest range, there is an openness and comfort to the sound. As we move up the scale, there is suddenly a sense that the very next note is not going to be able to be sung with the same comfort, much like the squeezing in of the neck of the hourglass. Then after a couple more notes going up the scale, we arrive in the middle register and everything is comfy again. So we go on our merry way up the scale and oh, my goodness, all of the sudden the voice starts to feel odd and almost like it has hit a ceiling. Many students are sure that they cannot proceed at this juncture, and this is where the statement—I can't sing high—is born.

As we sing from low to high, we encounter our various vocal registers. Everyone has at least three. In this discussion, I will refer to these as the chest, middle and head registers. Men will add an additional register known as their *falsetto*. In between each registration, you will find the passaggios, or transitions. These will be the two-to-three note passages that as we ascend the scale or descend the scale, in between each vocal register, feel odd, as if they don't want to coordinate like the other neighboring notes.

You can feel these by starting to hum on the lowest note you can sing. Then slowly move higher little by little until you notice an awkward feeling, like the next note you're going to sing doesn't quite want to work the same. As you ascend in pitch, the shift from your chest register to your middle register is a little tricky to feel, whereas if you are descending from the middle to chest, you will definitely notice a strange moment somewhere in the neighborhood of middle-C, D or E for women and an octave lower for men.

Now, if you continue singing higher through your middle register, you will come to a point where you feel like you can't or don't want to continue. This is typically the transition spot into your head register or what is known as the second passaggio.

I have noticed when my students are vocalizing, that the first passaggio (the one between the chest and middle registers) doesn't give them much trouble as they ascend, but this second one (between the middle and head registers) can pose a very serious challenge. In this conversation, it doesn't matter if you are male or female. All voices go through both of these transition areas and we all have to make adjustments in order to proceed to the highest parts of our voices.

What is interesting to me is that once you are past the passaggio itself, the voice begins to sing the notes above them with much more ease. If I can get a student through the odd feeling, there is always a look of surprise when the higher notes appear to be easier to them.

In working with the passaggios of many people of all ages and voice types over the years, I have found that when they are shown the pathway through these areas, 99 percent of them completely eliminate the conversation around limitations on high notes. Most all of my students have access to their full healthy range, which can be from one and a half to two and a half octaves and sometimes more!

One of my students, Sarah, was absolutely fearless in breaking through the constrictions she had placed upon herself. Once her voice was aligned, she was singing well above the highest note any soprano sings in any opera. She recently moved back to the U.S. West Coast, but in her last session with me vocalized to a high D above high D with ease and no constriction. The sound was extraordinary and very, very, very tiny.

I remember Edward, my bel canto teacher, calling those notes above high C the "money notes." He used to say that, if you can sing them consistently and well, you could get paid to do it! Obviously there are other important aspects to becoming a professional singer, but it never hurts to have full access to your vocal range.

Now, as I mentioned we don't normally notice our first passaggio as we ascend through the chest to middle register transition, but it is a very different experience if we are descending back down through it. So, when you are singing a song that sits predominantly in your middle range, and then are asked to go back down to your chest voice, you will notice an awkwardness again as you attempt to sing the two or three passaggio notes in-between. Suddenly the voice will feel like it doesn't quite know where to land.

A classic example of the challenge for women can be found in the song Susan Boyle made famous, "I Dreamed a Dream," from the musical *Les Miserables*. This song sits right in the first passaggio for most of the piece, and then suddenly descends down into the chest voice on the line, "But, the tigers come at night..." and if you aren't quite ready for it, your voice will feel like it is going right off the track. Often the voice will crackle as you attempt to sing the word—night.

This challenge may be corrected in one of two ways: we can keep in mind that the chest register is vocalized with much more speech-like energy, and articulation needs to become quite crisp and exact; the other method (to be discussed in detail in Lesson 13) involves maintaining a high lifted position in the face or cheek muscles as we descend to our lowest notes.

Lesson 10: Why To Avoid the Pitfalls of R's, Uh's, Aaaagh's and L's

Specifically, in our Americanized-English language there are four sounds that need to be addressed and either redirected or modified, as they interrupt and wreak havoc on our overall sound. The first of these sounds is the consonant R.

In other languages, the letter R is not pronounced the way we say it with a rather hard edge. In Italian, R's are either flipped or rolled and in most other languages the letter R is enunciated more smoothly. Notice sometime how a British person says R. Ending R's have a softer quality to them. Try saying the words river or deeper without closing your mouth. It will feel weird, but if we allow ourselves to sing this particular consonant, as we would say it, our ability to pitch or phonate the tone will stop. Nothing brings singing to a halt more abruptly than the letter R. So whenever I am faced with this letter, I will modify and opt to think about it more like a British person and keep the sound soft, leaving my mouth open as I finish the word.

The next sound that I always modify in my singing vocabulary is UH. This is the schwa sound found in words such as the, of, above, love, and because. The UH is challenging because of where we formulate the sound, so far back in our throats. If you pause for a moment and go through the list of words above, saying them slowly one at a time, you will notice what I mean.

When we go to sing the schwa sound, no matter where it occurs in a phrase, it will have a tendency to take us out of pitch and sound flat. Without thinking about it, this sound is virtually impossible to keep in tune. So the way I solve the problem is to always keep a mischievous smile on my face when I sing that sound. To a certain extent, by lifting like this, I place the sound forward more like an AH, thus avoiding the tendency for the schwa to move back into my throat. If I don't remember to lift however, I can almost be guaranteed that my ability to keep my pitch or tones in check will be thwarted.

The Aaaagh sound, as in the words cat, as, that, at and, am and than, also needs to be addressed. This sound tends to cause us to over-open our jaws. If you will say this phrase slowly, while looking in the mirror—I can take my cat in her crate and go see that vet—you may see for yourself what I am talking about. (Notice your mouth on the underlined words and see how wide you open it in relation to the rest of the phrase.)

This over-opening of the jaw is problematic for a number of reasons. The pitch will have a tendency to go out of tune, and your ability to control the rest of phrase that follows an Aaaagh sound will be tricky.

One solution for fixing this sound is to substitute EH for each Aaaagh encountered. For example, the word <u>can</u> becomes <u>ken</u>, the word <u>and</u> becomes <u>end</u>, and so forth. This modification helps keep the jaw more closed as you are singing and also helps the phrase remain more legato or smooth. Once this adjustment is practiced and felt, a singer can just think the EH sound and the voice will respond accordingly. Interestingly enough, this modification will sound perfectly natural to the listener, who will think you have used an Aaaagh.

The last of our problematic sounds is the L. If you finish a word on this sound, as in <u>well</u>, you can feel the tongue pull back into the throat, almost as if you are swallowing your tongue. This blocks the sound and interferes with your next breath preparation. A solution for this challenge is to cut off the L with only the tip of the tongue. You can practice this by saying EH and then bringing the tip of the tongue up to the hard palate, right behind the front teeth. This keeps the tongue forward in the mouth and prevents it from covering the opening in the back of the throat.

Of course, the challenge with all four of our problematic sounds is consistently remembering to make the modification required. When I am first learning a song, what I will do to assist myself is to go through the sheet music and mark or notate where these sounds occur. As I am working on the piece, the little notations will remind me to make the necessary adjustment when I am approaching the words that contain these pitfalls. All four of these letter-related challenges impact something we are going to talk about a bit later, the smoothness of your phrasing, known as the legato line.

Lesson 11: Articulation and Remembering the Speech Connection

We often forget that singing is connected to speaking. In the beginning of the book, I said that the elongation of vowels is the essence and definition of singing. As we all know, if it were that simple we would all be doing it in comfort without any effort. When we understand that our speech is connected to initiating and stabilizing good quality singing sound, we increase our effectiveness in achieving the ease we desire. So, how do we integrate this idea of speaking into our singing, once we have modified our challenging sounds and redirected our vowels to the Buzz spot?

Articulation is what we do when we talk. Crisp, clean, thoughtful articulation is what we tend to do when we think before we speak. Some cultures are known for this kind of precise speech, such as the British. Think about someone like Julie Andrews and her performances in *The Sound of Music* or *Mary Poppins*. The way in which she annunciated her words, both when speaking and singing, was so crisp and clear that in listening to her you understood every single word. This quick, precise initialization of sound is what gets the vocal mechanism engaged and stabilized quickly.

One of the things I notice in general about pop and contemporary music recordings is the frequency with which many singers scoop, slur or slide into their phrases. Instead of attacking a note right on pitch there will be a style of approach that has a singer articulate the first note of a phrase from below the actual pitch or tone. Listen carefully to any of your favorite singers in the more popular genres, and you will probably notice that the beginning word of many phrases will sound like there are two tones to it.

Slurring and sliding into phrases is the primary culprit behind our not being able to understand the words to many popular songs, for the uncontrolled start of the phrase keeps the singing mechanism slightly fuzzy for at least the first two or three notes and sometimes the entire phrase. Sometimes this particular issue is caused just by that little voice of doubt, saying we might not really know how to hit the first note. Sometimes it is a general lack of muscle preparation in the back of the throat and other times this challenge is exacerbated by too much airflow in the sound.

I usually ask beginning singers to forget what they hear on the radio until they understand more fully how to attack notes cleanly and get control of their initial attacks. I want them to experience the potential clarity of their own sound. I will always give the caveat that they can have their scooping card back once they can actually sing without slurring. The good news is that when you are stylistically scooping or slurring from a place of control your diction will become clearer and you will tend to be more accurate note-to-note, and more in tune overall.

Clean attacks: What does that mean? If you smile and crisply and precisely say a word you will feel a little edge or firmness to the initial sound, whether it is a word that starts with a vowel or consonant. When we precisely and quickly articulate the first word of a phrase like this, the vocal folds coordinate really fast, stabilizing the pitch quickly. At this point, you will hear and feel an almost speech-like quality to your singing sound.

Believe it or not, this precise gentle articulation on the initial word of the sentence makes phrases that have been difficult to sing become much easier to manage, almost as if we have gotten on a little train track of control. Clean attacks are also particularly helpful when dealing with passaggios, which we discover later in our process together.

There are a couple of instances where I will consistently articulate the word with an even firmer attack, and both of those happen to be vowel-related. When the word I, for example, appears in a sentence, I will re-attack that sound as if I am saying it on pitch. This re-articulation helps re-anchor any phrase and allows for clearer understanding of the words. The other example of when I am particularly careful with annunciation is when a phrase begins with a word that starts with a vowel, like end or open or air.

When I breathe, I will do my breath prep by thinking AH and stretching the back of my throat into position, and then when I start to sing, almost say the word to begin the phrase. You may feel that little edge to the sound when you start the line. This edge will be softened as we begin to feel our control of the phrase and can be articulated quite gently with the same superior results.

For me, the most important note of the phrase is the first one for, if articulated properly, it allows you to sing the rest of the notes of the phrase with less effort. This does take a little practice, as we are thinking about so many things when we are first getting started. But for now, just put this piece of information in the back of your mind and as we go forward we will pull it all together.

For purposes of clarification, let me add this piece: when you do your breath prep on an AH and feel the stretch in the back of the throat, the place where you feel that stretch is called the pharynx. If you exhale again and think E, you will feel a shift in the shape back there to a more horizontal position and if you do it again thinking O, you will notice another change in the muscles.

The pharyngeal muscles, that area where you feel the muscles stretching into place at the back and top of the throat is where the vowels are made or articulated. When we initiate a gentle, yet firm, precise vowel sound, we may feel a small engagement there. This is not the same as a hard glottal attack, which you feel deeper down in the throat and will feel more forced. As we proceed in our journey towards ease of vocal production, just know that the more you become aware of energizing and sustaining your musculature in the singing process, while developing the necessary support in the body, the less you will feel in your throat overall.

Chapter 5. Lift, Lift, Lift

Chapter 5. Lift, Lift, Lift

Lesson 12: Where To Put Your "Cheshire Cat" Grin

In the beginning of the book, we talked about the Bow-and-Arrow breathing approach and how that allows for a stretch to occur in the back of throat, which in turn creates a mini-amphitheater. To refresh that feeling, let's do the breath prep. Remember to think AH and inhale slowly. Right where you feel that stretch in the back of the throat is where we now want to focus our attention.

Many singers talk about an inner smile, where this stretch on an AH sound, lifts what is called the soft palate. There are two palates in our mouths, a hard one and a soft one. If we place our tongue behind our upper front teeth and press upward, we will feel the hard palate. Moving our tongues backward along the roof of our mouths, we will notice we come to a spongy area, where we can make a clucking sound like we did as kids. This is the soft palate.

For optimal singing position, this soft palate is raised. If you lift up your eyebrows, you can feel that area lifting internally. The challenge is keeping it in place. If I say to a student, "raise your soft palate," she can do it by lifting the eyebrows or inhaling on the Bow-and-Arrow principle, but keeping the palate up throughout a complete phrase becomes a challenge.

Some teachers describe lifting the soft palate by using images of a small apple in the mouth or an egg. These images pose two challenges for the singer. The first is that, although we can picture an egg or small apple as we inhale, continuing to sustain that image throughout an entire phrase becomes challenging when we start to articulate. The other problematic piece, for me, is that we will almost automatically lose our forward vowel control, and the sounds we make will become darker and farther back in the mouth.

Just for fun, think of the egg or apple in the mouth, breathe in, and then try to talk while maintaining that feeling. You will notice the awkwardness you feel and the affected sound, a bit like Julia Childs. So this is where I use the "Cheshire cat" smile, like the character from "Alice's Adventures in Wonderland" by Lewis Carroll. This image of a big toothy grin will become helpful to us as singers, as we establish an engaged and stabilized high soft palate.

Picture that grin, literally from ear to ear. Place the points of the smile in either ear and, feeling the stretch of the grin across the back of the throat, you will feel your inner smile lift. This image, especially when initiated at the beginning of every phrase, as you do your breath prep, will begin to exercise these internal muscles. Sometimes I will joke with my students and say, "Imagine you are using clothes pins to hold up that smile right at the level of your ears."

As you strengthen your ability to stay engaged this way, you should notice that the inner smile is much easier to maintain throughout a whole sentence. But like any other muscle training, it requires some time and practice to remain consistent.

Now why is keeping the soft palate lifted so important? This is the back of your amphitheater. Remember when we were talking about the way that the voice works? The pitch is created at the larynx, the vowels are articulated at the pharynx (top back of the throat) and then the sound is directed outwards towards the teeth and little spot right under your nose. So, now picture this spongy area we just identified as the soft palate.

If it is completely relaxed, it becomes essentially like a normal ceiling in a room, flat and un-energized. So imagine, here's comes a lovely tone from the larynx and a wondrous vowel sound gets made by the pharynx and suddenly this fabulous sound hits a flat wall. It essentially dies and dulls right on the spot. There is nowhere for that sound to go but right into muscle tissue.

84

So, we create another lovely tone accompanied by a terrific vowel and this time our soft palate is curved and lifted. The sound instead of running into a wall has a curved area to ride over and once directed up and over the palate, the sound just happens to be in line to go right to the spot under the nose.

Think of it this way: without the curve of the soft palate in the upward position, your mini-amphitheater has really bad acoustics! This muscular piece of the puzzle is probably the most critical of all the pieces in terms of sound quality. I can make an argument for the breath support being essential and when we get to the next lift—the frontal lift—I get very impassioned about that one too, but pretty much all voice teachers would agree that without the engagement of the soft palate, the whole singing thing doesn't work very well.

When a student needs a funny little reminder to keep this area lifted, I often say, "Now, breathe in, and remember your party in the back!"

Lesson 13: Cheeks Up, Everybody!

So, in that last analysis of the soft palate lift, I mentioned that I get pretty excited about another area for us to lift. This one comes out of my bel canto understanding and engages the area I call the Buzz. This forward lift creates the possibility of sound stabilization so profound that whether used by an individual or in a group or chorus setting, the number one problem with singing, remaining in tune, becomes effortless.

A set of muscles that Americans, in particular, sometimes need to exercise a bit more are their cheeks! Smiling, perhaps due to the stress of our lifestyles or in some cases, the more reserved parts of the country in which we live, is not something we all do on a regular basis. Of course, Italians also are not always happy; however, when they speak their faces are engaged and energized — so much so that we automatically identify the whole Italian culture with the word "animated"!

In order to emulate them (which I believe helps with our singing ease) we need to practice this one particular lift. It helps us to feel and place our vowels in the brighter, more forward position and, once mastered, will stabilize our overall sound. If I were to say that one piece of this whole crazy puzzle transformed my life as a singer, it is this lift.

So, how do we practice this piece? By taking our two index fingers and creating a horizontal line right under our nose, pressing in slightly, we will once again feel the indentation between our gums and cheeks. While keeping the fingers there, imagine that the cheek muscles are now lifting up off the gum line, right beside the nose, almost like we have smelled something stinky. If you look in the mirror, you will see an engagement of the muscles happening right in that Buzz spot, or what I also call the forward lift.

In truth, this engagement is almost more akin to a sneer, but of course, that is not particularly attractive for performing. So, to make it look pretty and for initial purposes of practicing, you can create this same feeling by making a small mischievous smile, showing your teeth. If you will keep your cheeks engaged, even though it feels awkward and fake, and then begin singing, you may notice right away that the sound stays more even and in tune.

Part of the reason this works so well is that it sends a kinesthetic message to the brain. If the lift is maintained, your mind will direct the vowel sounds to this little area under the nose and keep them there, not letting them return to where they naturally resonate when we speak. In essence we are tricking the body to reorient these sounds to vibrate or resonate in this new spot. I like to refer to this as relocating our vowels to one-condo-on-one-floor-with-one-door-and-one-key. All of our vowel sounds can live in this one place, once we are aware of the forward location and get accustomed to feeling when our vowel sounds slip back.

If you are someone who watches competitive singing shows or notices famous singers, you will start to realize that the good ones are always lifted in their faces. If they are not actually smiling, you will see their cheeks are engaged and often their smile lines will be apparent. If you watch those singers that lose pitch quality or tuning on *American Idol, X Factor, The Voice* or another singing talent show, you may notice that they are either not lifted at all, or that they drop randomly as they are singing.

I will say that this lift is the most difficult to do consistently. The English language in particular, and the way we all speak culturally, does not require us to smile. Given the other stress-related challenges we are facing these days or even this cultural appropriateness filter, this animated way of being may go against our grain to some degree and feel incredibly awkward and exposed. But, if you can put that aside for the moment and, just for the sake of your voice, try to stay lifted, you can fight the urge to drop and disengage.

By the way, I know that it is going to feel really weird, as if you are at a cocktail party or function where you feel completely uncomfortable and are managing to put on a fake smile just to get through it. For some, this forward lift will feel that bizarre. But, the payoff for getting your face engaged is huge.

We will talk pretty soon about using the mirror to help us sustain our lifts and find our way to balance with our voices. This lift is one example of why being willing to look at yourself is so important. If you don't look in the mirror to see if you are smiling or engaged in the face, you may not be able to feel it. I can't tell you how many times I will need to repeat to a student in the studio, "check your forward lift."

I would say that my own personal investment in this understanding is nothing short of four years' worth of total vowel therapy. Since then, I have gotten so used to maintaining this engagement that my vowels really never drop into my throat or fall back, and this stability of sound affords me clear, effortless, consistent singing. As a side benefit, I am able to play with my students going in and out of foreign accents with ease, helping to demonstrate these principles. Someone was watching me coach a group recently and said, "You lift all the time. You are doing it when you speak and you do it when you sing. I never saw you drop once."

This is not something I ever learned before my bel canto training. So, I am asking you to really give this piece some extra attention. I daresay that you will never go too far with this lift, with the only exception being if you happen to have lots of jaw tension, which is an issue we will address separately.

For those of you that might be unsure of yourself at this point, just know that at the end of the book we will have information on how you can warm up with me online, if you want to check yourself against my muscle placement. You will be able to watch my demonstration videos on YouTube.com, work with me on PowHow.com in a group session or perhaps even have the ability to Skype with me privately, where I will demonstrate this forward engagement and give you exercises to strengthen your Buzz, where you can feel the sensations in your own face; you'll then be able to mimic me and reinforce the behavior.

This additional coaching might be just the thing to help you get past the feeling of awkwardness and silliness. Frankly this lift also has another side benefit. Not only will this help your singing, but also, if you smile regularly, it can't help but have you feel better about life in general.

Joy is very catchy! And in this particular case, the adage "Fake it 'til you make it!" is well worth the effort.

Lesson 14: My Son, the Wide-Mouthed Frog, and Julia Child

When my son was very young, he would sit at the top of the stairs and observe me teaching some of my students. With the younger ones, we would often do silly things like the wide-mouth frog exercise. That is the one where the mouth is opened very wide on each of the words in this phrase: "I'm—a—wide-mouthed—frog."

If I forgot to have a younger student do that exercise on any given day, my son would be sure to remind me of it later. It showed me that even at a young age, he was already paying attention to what his mom was doing, and saying!

When we sing in English, we sometimes have to be mindful to not open our mouths too wide in order to keep the sound legato and stable. Certain people, though, have so much jaw-tension that opening their mouth at all is a challenge. In these cases, I will usually have a student hold his jaw very gently, by putting their hands on both sides of their face, while we are doing vocal exercises. Sometimes, like an actor warming up his facial muscles, I will have the student do this wide-mouthed frog exercise two or three times just to bring awareness to this area of the mouth and jaw, even though we will never be hinging our jaw that wide when we sing.

For some reason, when we incorporate the gentle support of the hands on the jaw and sides of the face, the muscles almost immediately relax. As we mentioned in Lesson 8 on the tongue and jaw, this can also be done without vocalizing, while watching television or sitting at a desk. Just allowing the jaw to move slowly up and down can help to release tension in the face. Remember that when it comes to singing, there is good tension and bad tension.

Any tension that causes pain or constriction is considered negative, but the lifts that we have talked about earlier can also be seen as a kind of positive tension or suspension. So, it really does come down to noticing what is beneficial for vocal production and what is contrary to the process. There are several oppositional energies in singing such as lifting and lowering at the same time, for example the soft palate lifts and the larynx lowers, and in order to feel consistent sound, we need to deal with these kinds of challenges.

Remember back in the beginning, when we spoke of goofing around and playing with foreign accents as being beneficial to finding our true voice? Well, in bel canto, in addition to the bright forward vowel production, we also want to exercise and reinforce our inner amphitheater, which is the imaginary shell-like structure in the back of the throat and mouth, so that our overall resonance reverberates within us as a stable instrument.

This openness or height to the structure of the inside of our mouths, maintained by a high soft palate, allows sound to resonate properly. To feel that stretch in yet another way, sometimes I will have a student pretend that she is Julia Child in the kitchen and imitate her very unusual accent, in yet another opportunity to goof around and create an understanding of the vocal mechanism. After the release of *Julie & Julia*, almost everyone has had some access to her unique speaking sound, which is very open and can sound rather dark and even a bit hooty, like an owl. This one vocal exercise, done while playing in the kitchen for full effect, allows for a nice stretch in the back of the throat.

As I mentioned, in order to fully understand how the singing instrument works, there are a number of dualities that we have to contend with, sort of like the image of a helicopter moving in many directions at once. Remember, we are an actual physical acoustic instrument, like a guitar or violin. The only difference is that our instrument is made of soft tissue, and is more like gel than wood. As you can imagine, if a guitar or violin turned to gel while being strummed, you would not get a very good sound out of it. That, in essence, is the problem we deal with as human beings trying to vibrate or resonate good tone.

The concept of *chiaroscuro* helps us interpret how the bel canto principles work in resonance and vocal production. Chiaroscuro means light/dark, like shaded pencil artwork. In the bel canto orientation, the light concept has to do with the bright forward vowels and the dark refers to the open, rounded, and lifted musculature that essentially sustains the structure of our instrument.

By getting used to holding up the high, rounded ceiling of our amphitheater, and always re-engaging that feeling on each breath prep before a phrase, we have the opportunity to maintain the integrity of our instrument so that beautiful sound can freely emerge. I often say to my students that the voice is rarely, if ever, the problem; it is more likely the instability of the structure either collapsing or morphing the sound.

By practicing the stretch in the back of the throat in a variety of ways, we will find the particular thought process that works best for us for sustaining this high structure. Sometimes in singing and learning how to work with our voices, a teacher will have to come up with several different ways to explain the same thing in order to find the key to unlocking a particular student's mind and thought process. This is exactly what we are doing now. So whether the using image of the breath prep or the Bow-and-Arrow stretch, or goofing around in the kitchen like Julia works best, it's your choice.

Lesson 15: The Car Salesman and the Beauty Queen

When we start to put all of the pieces together, you may notice that there are times where the frontal lift and the higher orientation of the roof of the mouth has a fake feeling to it. This really has to do with the fact that many of us tend to speak in a very relaxed fashion, where our facial muscles do not actively engage and stay animated. All of these exercises, so far, are attempting to rectify that, and stimulate a more energized and effective posture for singing.

But, until we are used to the musculature staying in these positions, singing may feel inconsistent. If I get into the lifted position, hold steady and then start talking, I almost immediately feel as if I am speaking with a foreign accent, without even trying. As funny as this sounds, it is as if the problems associated with the closed Americanized-English language automatically dissipate.

My students find it humorous that I can go from accent to accent without really trying, but it is mostly due to the fact that maintaining our faces this way makes it harder to complete words the way we normally do, closing down final sounds, especially when we are lifted to this degree. The problem sounds, like R, UH, and Aaaagh almost immediately go away.

The fake feeling that accompanies these lifted positions may make you feel like you have become the stereotypical cartoonish car salesman or beauty queen, or as if you are at a party where you don't know anyone, but have to be friendly and polite non-stop. Remember that this may feel very weird, especially for those of us not accustomed to smiling a lot. Eventually this fake sensation will feel more normal, as the muscles themselves get stronger and we become less self-conscious while singing.

Suffice it to say, engaging the musculature every time we breathe creates the most dramatic results in our singing. As I mentioned previously, it becomes imperative that we get the muscles energized and stabilized in order for our voices to resonate properly. By focusing on doing this on every single phrase we sing, we begin to develop consistency throughout whole songs.

I truly believe that our individual voices are already there, waiting to emerge. In essence I am not teaching you how to sing, I am teaching you how to get out of the way of your singing.

Lesson 16: You're Crazy If You Think I Can Sing High and Other Myths

When new students come into the vocal studio, I usually determine what they already know by asking a few questions. Typically, breath support carries with it a number of misnomers and vague concepts that we then talk about and clarify. When I ask what the student's goals or objectives are, they almost always reply that they would like to increase their range and have more high notes.

Once we are doing the warm-ups, we will get to a spot where I look at the student's face and see a clear sign of panic. Usually it looks like a furrow between the eyes or someone who is about to squeeze their eyes closed. I will stop the lesson and ask what the thought was right in that moment and it will always be the same, "I don't think I can sing that note."

Believe it or not, this really always happens at the same spot for everyone, the first note of their second transition or passaggio. This one note feels so different and so uncomfortable for most people that it will stop singers in their tracks for just long enough to throw a proverbial monkey wrench into the process. It is my job to demonstrate to the student that if they will trust me for just a few moments and try what I am asking them to try, I can get them through this passageway. Once through, another whole range of notes becomes available to the singer, known as the head register. But the curious thing is that once we are in that upper head register, those high notes don't feel as hard to sing, as the notes of the second passaggio, or transition, itself.

For most high sopranos, the highest notes are not their main challenge. The middle notes tend to be more difficult. This shows up when a singer can start the warm-up in the lower register or chest voice and everything is pretty comfortable. But when that soprano hits the first passaggio or passageway, all of a sudden the voice seems to weaken, and the singer doesn't seem to be able to get any power for several notes. If I can keep them going through their discomfort at this juncture, there will be another point, usually as we are coming through the second passaggio, where suddenly the voice reappears and the singer relaxes again.

This particular challenge is normally created because there is too much pressure put on the very lowest notes and the weight from that part of the voice when it gets to around the "D" above middle-C (or the first passaggio) becomes too big or heavy for that part of the voice and the instrument appears to give out.

Two solutions exist. One is to reduce the amount of pressure, weight or volume to begin with, while increasing support, and the other is to engage the forward lift and be slightly more articulate through those beginning middle register notes, allowing the voice to anchor more cleanly, with a bit of speech-like energy. A combination of all of the above will certainly guarantee better access to the transitional area.

The other thing we can look at is our breath control in this area of the voice. When we get into trouble, we tend to try to push sound out and inadvertently press too much air through the vocal cords, which destabilizes them. Imagine two saloon doors right next to each other, which no one has gone through for a while. Suddenly a brisk wind comes up, some cowboy comes striding through, and those doors won't stop swinging open.

Your vocal cords, as you remember, oscillate or vibrate together with sustained, gentle air pressure. Any abrupt or aggressive airflow through them can suddenly push them open and it takes a second to reestablish their coordinated effort. By keeping the ribs out and engaged and by not over-blowing air through them, we can articulate a nice long phrase with less effort. One way to address high notes that don't want to coordinate is to hold back air, almost imagining that you are inhaling on those notes, instead of pushing at them.

Try this: inhale, expanding your ribs and engaging them gently, and then hold your breath. Begin your phrase and continue to feel like you are holding your breath. See if you can feel the difference in the ease as you maneuver up to your higher notes. Remember that once we articulate, air is flowing, so we aren't actually holding our breath. But, the very small stream of air that is coming through the cords themselves is not enough to disrupt their continued coordination.

When you hear a singer sing a clear upper tone with virtually no air in the sound, they are controlling their airflow, while maintaining and leaning into the inner sustained pressure they are feeling. It is really easy to do this once you have felt the experience of holding the energy this way, but until that time, it can seem a bit elusive.

There are, of course, those students who come into the studio with the belief that they do not have much of a range at all. They experience comfort on only a few notes and the rest, both low and high, are seemingly unavailable. This is generally a sign of one thing—the voice is out of alignment. The truth is, most of us aren't lined up properly to begin with, and until our attention is directed as to how to make that happen, we are pretty much clueless on how to proceed. There is nothing worse than knowing a problem exists and not having any scnsc as to how to fix it.

Imagine a pyramid. It is larger and weightier on the bottom, at the base, and narrows to a point on the top. With the voice, there is a need to narrow or brighten the voice as we move up the scale from bottom to top. It's as if we need to gradually remove some of the weight from the voice, in order to navigate through the passaggios and create one continuous line.

As soon as I start this ascent, singing from my lowest notes, I am almost immediately aware of shaving off the heaviness that naturally occurs in the bottom of my range, as I try to maneuver up to the top of my *tessitura,* or high notes. After doing this for several years myself, I no longer feel the passaggios at all. This, of course, takes some time. But, if you start slowly and just become aware when you are pushing or feeling the need to get louder on any particular note or phrase, you will find that you can tune into where this additional weight is bothersome for you.

Once there is an understanding in the mind about the musculature—how to lift the soft palate and get the cheeks in a more energized position—combined with maintaining bright, forward Italian vowels, and proper breath support/control, this gradual weight transfer happens almost automatically. Once trained to do so, a healthy voice will be able to sing a full range of notes from the chest voice to the head register without feeling a lot of effort or change from register to register and the experience of having one voice vs. three or four, occurs naturally as a result of this effort.

Integrating this process can be slow, as each person has a unique set of puzzle pieces, mechanical issues or muscle tensions that have to be identified and then adjusted. But, once overcome with some diligent practice, you may never go back to being out of alignment again.

Chapter 6: Mirror, Mirror in Your Hall: Easy Ways To Improve Quickly

Lesson 17: The Eye-Mind Connection

The hardest thing for me to get a student to do is to look in a mirror while practicing. Many of us tend to feel awkward about looking at ourselves to begin with, never mind while we are singing. But the reality is that without the aid of a mirror, we can't feel what we are doing effectively in the beginning of this process. Even seasoned students that are used to me reminding them to lift or to create the fake feeling with their teeth showing will be surprised when I say in a session that they are dropped. They think they are energized and lifted, but when they look in the mirror they will see that this is not the case.

I believe that this happens because we are accustomed to speaking in a different way. Our speech habits directly impact our vocal habits as singers and, unless we are willing to look in the mirror to see these distinctions (particularly when we get into trouble), the body will inadvertently drop and send the sound to the more comfortable or familiar backspace in the throat.

You may already know that you don't hear yourself accurately anyway. For some of us, we are so used to hearing the sound as heavy and dark that when we move the voice forward, it feels as if we aren't working very hard and, in essence, that we are not really singing. In my mouth, I feel my voice vibrating mostly from my cheekbones forward. So, if you are used to feeling a big sound in your head, be prepared for a different experience when you move it to the front towards the Buzz area. What we want to remember is that what our listeners hear is more important than feeling powerful inside our heads. We may actually be covering up our voices when we manufacture a sound and become dark and heavy. It may feel good to you, but to the rest of the world, you may not sound in tune.

When we are willing to look at ourselves as we practice and keep the musculature in the new, more effective, position, eventually eye-mind coordination takes over and the body memorizes the new feelings on a cellular level. Just know that there will be a point where the coordination of all these little pieces integrates and feels more natural.

One little tip I can give you in this department—when you look in the mirror, focus your attention on your mouth. Don't look directly into your eyes for this exercise. For some reason we can get distracted and uncomfortable looking into our own eyes. There is a time for that particular exercise, that perhaps has more to do with acknowledging and recognizing our spiritual presence, but for purposes of singing, I believe that by focusing on your mouth, you will have an easier time dealing with this aspect of your practice.

So once again, here is my primary reason that you want to be willing to look—all of these adjustments will take less time to integrate into your body. Therefore, it will cost less, both in time and money, as well as reduce your frustration level. From experience, I can say that there are definitely moments where learning to sing effectively can be a bit frustrating. Getting your body to do what you want it to do when it is used to doing something very different can be aggravating. So please don't be afraid to do the one thing that will exponentially help you improve—look at your mouth!

Lesson 18: Putting the Mouth in Proper Perspective

So, when we look in the mirror, what are we looking for? Remember when we were talking about the two types of lifts, one external and one internal, the Buzz spot and the inner smile? The external or forward lift is created when we energize our cheek muscles up off the gum line. This is where we will feel our Buzz when we hum in this position. It is here that you will notice the muscles right next to the nose indent ever so slightly.

This position is one that needs to stay stable and present at all times. When this little muscular engagement consistently remains in place, the sounds you sing will be more consistent as well. Unfortunately, when we start vocalizing on lower notes our body decides that we don't need this lift to accommodate these particular notes, so, the frontal lift tends to drop, and you will feel the sound go to a much darker place, almost as if it were swallowed. In some cases you will actually feel the sound go into the throat and, if you are low enough, notes will become very difficult to articulate and sing at all.

One of the weird things about singing in this energized way is that the lower you go in your range, the higher you really want to feel your lift. There is an oppositional energy, almost like an elevator going up at the same time we are descending. I literally feel myself hold my sound up in my mouth, as I go lower. If I don't do this, my pitch sags and my placement goes back into my throat. If you are feeling sound in your throat, this is occurring. I never feel anything in mine.

So when you look in the mirror as you sing a descending line or move into your chest voice, notice what your face wants to do and see if you can fight the feeling of letting the sound drop back, just by keeping the cheeks engaged up. If in doubt, smile! For me, nothing ever descends, every note we make is always going up, like we are creating a kind of anti-gravity.

Now, when you are watching yourself in the mirror and you see your mouth want to droop or drop, try lifting it so that you can see your teeth again. As you are singing a song, you may notice that the face will want to go to different positions along the way, depending on the vowel sound you are singing and where you are in your range. Remembering to keep the cheeks up and the upper teeth showing a bit (although you may feel somewhat restricted in your movement, as if you have a little straightjacket stabilizing your mouth), you will notice that the sound will stay more even and smooth.

Another thing to look for in the mirror is what I call the light-behind-the-eyes feeling or your inner ditz. Imagine that you don't have a thought in your brain. This may take some of that good old goofing around energy to get to for some of us (I know it does for me), but feeling like we are a little ditzy gives us an imaginary internal sensation of height.

When looking in the mirror while doing this, you will notice that your eyes will also appear a little more engaged, like your outer smile has extended all the way up to your forehead. Holding that feeling while singing is another way to increase space in our mouths, engaging the soft palate and back of our throats, which again allows for clearer, more even resonance.

This high internal feeling also has other stabilizing benefits. As we talk about vertical movement from low to high notes and back again, this back-energized space or inner smile helps us keep the sound more legato and even. I will often tell a student to always breathe in for his very highest notes in a sentence and maintain that space throughout the phrase. This allows us to be prepared for whatever note is coming our way. So when you do your breath prep, imagine the AH and engage the inner smile, then maintain that structure.

Once again, it is helpful to use a mirror while thinking about that inner smile going from ear to ear, because when that lift is engaged inside the vocal mechanism, you can actually see it on your face and it will look like light or joy in your eyes. Memorizing what this feels like as we look at our reflection helps us to integrate the lifted musculature into our singing sound. So for me, looking in the mirror really is the fastest way to great results!

Lesson 19: The Fastest Way To Great Results

Let's review some of the pieces of the puzzle that we need to think about, as we prepare to sing a phrase.

✓ Checking our posture, we notice that our head is centered over our body with our chin not lifting up. The back of our neck is lengthened. Our chest is lifted and ready to engage the ribs on inhalation.

✓ Hearing the first pitch or tone in our mind, we inhale using the image of the Bow-and-Arrow preparation, remembering to think AH and in one fluid movement we lift the cheeks, roof of the mouth and soft palate or inner smile in preparation for making sound.

✓ While keeping the ribcage engaged and open, articulate, quickly and firmly, the first word of the phrase, without hesitation, allowing the lower jaw to release slightly, but not hyper-extending it.

✓ While maintaining forward and internal lifts, remain on the target or open, pure vowel sound of each syllable until you have to articulate the next syllable or word. Try not to allow diphthongs to close down too soon. On sustained tones avoid the final consonant of each syllable until you are ready to articulate the next one. Movement should go vowel-to-vowel-to vowel, with quick, precise consonant production.

✓ Remember that R's and L's will cause you to close down the sound and the throat, so keep your R's soft and your L's created with only the tip of the tongue.

✓ Note: When you are singing at this stage, you may feel like the sound is incomplete and, when taken to the extreme, might even feel as if you are using a bit of a European accent, but to the listener the singing will sound completely natural, with clear, understandable diction.

Chapter 7: Properly Program Your Mind's Software

Lesson 20: Pushing, Pulling, and Kinesthetic Learning

As we set off to become effective singers, it helps to understand that singing is about setting up a space in our own bodies that supports good vocal production, and then allowing the voice to vibrate or resonate properly. When our mind thinks it doesn't understand how to do something, our brain tends to take over, and then tries to make it happen—sort of like throwing something aimlessly at a wall. Ultimately this creates a kind of "push me—pull you" experience. Results are more difficult when we start stabbing in the dark trying to make sound, especially when we are trying to sing in the more challenging parts of our vocal range.

Often, our first instinct is to try and project sound using some amount of force. Unfortunately, this causes us to push a lot of air through the vocal cords on our first attack or articulation. Sometimes, if you really focus in on this piece, you will notice that your first note or two will feel somewhat unstable or very diffused. Too much air is almost like adding too much water to a package of Kool-Aid. In that case, as you can imagine, you end up with colored water. With our voices, adding lots of air lessens our ability to sustain clear tones.

As we can't hear ourselves very accurately, feeling the voice resonate properly becomes very important. So, we will want to tune into the sound from a different perspective. By noticing what we feel when the sound is correct, combined with our practice of looking in the mirror, we will have come to a place where we can self-evaluate, at least to some degree, what might be going on in the musculature when we are having problems or facing transitional challenges. As a side note, you can actually hear what you sound like if you record yourself practicing on your IPod, IPhone or small MP3 player, which I do recommend.

Hearing our voices often brings up its own set of issues, such as the potential negative evaluation that might have been caused by looking in the mirror. But when we are really committed to creating great sound, if we can remove our self-judgment and become a little more detached, not taking things so personally, we can more effectively evaluate our sound quality and impact it in very positive ways, without having to engage in vocal manipulation or mimicking other people's sounds.

One thing that helps stop the mind from randomly trying to manipulate the sound is to incorporate kinesthetic learning into the process. So, sometimes I may suggest physical movements to support our integration and learning. Over the years, kids I have worked with have taught me that moving the body, an arm, or hand during certain exercises or while singing a song helps draw a picture for the mind and, lo and behold, the voice follows the movement. An interesting piece emerges where, depending on how I move my body, my voice will actually follow that energy. If it is jerky and uneven, my voice will sound jerky and uneven. If I move my hand smoothly, my voice will maintain its legato line.

You can try it right now by drawing a straight line with your hand in front of you. Try and keep your movement very even. Now draw that straight line in front of you and hum a note. Make the line very smooth, slow and even, and as you do, you will hear your humming stay smooth, too. Now hum a note while making a bumpy line. It will be very difficult to control the pitch and have it remain steady.

Being physically aware of the body will help us as we start to work with the voice. Occasionally I may have you push on a wall, pull on your hands like the old fashioned diva stance, or just draw the shape of a phrase you are trying to sing in order to have you feel your voice, not just hear it. The more you are able to feel what you are doing, as opposed to just trying to listen to your voice, the easier it will be to sing consistently. This is especially true when we are in difficult acoustic situations, where our hearing is impeded. Feeling what is happening inside your body, when the voice is working properly, will help you to repeat the correct behaviors.

When it comes to recording your voice, in the beginning, be aware that you may not always like your sound. This is a natural part of finding your true voice. Think of it this way—we have to discover the boundaries, or parts of the voice where we go a little too far over the edge, in order to know where those places are. So expect a few amazingly bad notes. In my search for my own well-balanced voice, I would say I hit well over a couple thousand awful notes, maybe more. This is not only okay, it is also important.

To a certain extent, getting over ourselves, and our judgments, is one of the most helpful things we can do for our process. Erroneous negative thoughts get in the way of making beautiful sounds and prevent us from breaking through our fears and concerns about releasing the voice. So go ahead and make mistakes, notice them, and know that if you do so, they will start to stop happening. As in the rest of life, those things that we resist looking at are the things that tend to perpetuate.

Lesson 21: How Your Thoughts Work Against You

The most difficult piece of the singing puzzle is unwinding the undesirable and unproductive thoughts that are programmed into our minds. Because most of these thoughts are quite old and come from early childhood memories, they are difficult to identify and dispel at times. Sometimes they were put into our minds via an unconscious comment made by a third party, like a teacher or parent.

In my belief, a single erroneous thought sends a singer down the path of doubt, which never ends well! These thoughts could be things like: "I can't sing," "I can't sing high notes," "I'm afraid I am going to be flat or sharp," "My voice is terrible," or "I don't know what I am doing."

The problem with these thoughts is somewhat obvious, but the impact of the thoughts on the singer goes far beyond their apparent negative implications. The voice of doubt tends to insert itself right between the breath prep and articulation. In that split second, one stray thought can send a note completely off-course, and I compare it to any other practice, like golf or martial arts or meditation. Being centered and in a space of being right-minded for singing, means no negative thoughts allowed.

But how do we dispel them, if we believe them to be true? Just like anything else, it takes practice. It takes time to unwind thoughts that prevent our voices from emerging with ease. As a negative thought is noticed, you can take a moment to write it down. Then put it aside while you are warming up or doing some singing.

Later, when you have a few moments, go back to that thought. Ask yourself how old you were when that thought first came into being. Once you have identified an age, ask for more information. Do you remember who said it to you? Or what the circumstances were, that caused that one thought to be embraced by your mind? Get as much information as you can from your memories and write them down. Then leave it again for a bit.

Sometime later, maybe after a week or so, go back and look again. See if any more information has come to you about that particular thought. Now, ask yourself the honest question…is this thought true? Or is it a belief that exists because of someone's unconscious communication? Is it something I am willing to put aside, and let go of in this new moment in my life? If not, put the thought away and let more time elapse and repeat the exercise again. But if the answer is yes, I am ready to let go of this thought/belief, let's walk through releasing it together.

If it was a thought created by another person's communication that was unkind or unconscious, I would like you to consciously choose to forgive them for that. Because chances are they didn't know any better, and it was said in a moment without the understanding that their comment would linger with you this long. And as we have discovered in this journey together, most of us, even teachers, don't realize that even when the sound is problematic, it isn't personal, it is caused by our language, which can affect anyone.

So, take a moment and see them, speaking out loud that you forgive them and that you are letting the thought go. Then take that paper and destroy it. Tear it up into little pieces and throw it away. As silly as this exercise may seem, it takes back your power and resumes accountability for your experience: both very empowering actions.

Now as you are singing, if that thought returns, you then can say to it, "Thank you for protecting me all these years, by preventing me from reaching out and risking, but I no longer need you to do so."

I call this dialing down the volume of negativity in your mind; and, as you can imagine, the practice of eliminating ineffective thinking works for all areas of life. But with singing, it becomes critical, for your voice wants to emerge and feel safe in doing so. Without releasing these beliefs, sometimes the emotional body will not let us communicate and, in my experience, your singing may become very challenged and difficult.

Lesson 22: Why Not Give the Mind Something Better To Do?

So now that we have cleared out the negative thoughts, what is the mind to do? Focus on those principles, those pieces of the pragmatic puzzle that will give you great results! So if we were in a session together, these would be the things I would be listening for and repeating back to you to do:

- ✓ *Breathe*—remembering that you want to inhale slowly and gently.
- ✓ *Lift*—as you inhale, you are preparing the muscles in your mouth to sing.
- ✓ *Engage*—maintain expanded ribcage and lifted cheeks throughout phrase.
- ✓ *Maintain*—inner smile, space in back of throat stays open to create room.
- ✓ *Articulate*—crisply, cleanly and gently, while sustaining ribs and small airflow.
- ✓ *Legato*—pure open vowel sound on each syllable, avoiding pitfalls of diphthongs.
- ✓ *Intention*—keep your energy on the sound thinking about the arc of the phrase.
- ✓ *Arc*—Use a kinesthetic hand motion to draw a picture for the voice and body.

As singers, our individual challenges vary from person to person, mainly because our body types are different and how we are built determines what type of voice we have—how heavy or light it is, how flexible we are, and how high or low we can go. So, you may find that one or two of the above principles may be more difficult to integrate into your thought process. Just remember it takes some time to coordinate all of these pieces at once. So what I normally suggest is that when you practice, focus on one aspect at a time. Pretty soon you will notice you can think about two things at once, then suddenly three, four, five and then one day, you will realize you are holding all eight thoughts in your mind at one time.

Singing well is a bit complicated in the beginning. The beauty of this work is that over time there is muscular and mental integration that takes place. One day you will notice that parts of the process are just easier. You may not even realize when that happens. But, depending on the kind of emotional blocks we might be carrying and how willing we are to focus the mind away from these things, the possibility exists to create an effortless, great sound!

Chapter 8: Principles of Bel Canto That Help You Sing With Ease

Chapter 8: Principles of Bel Canto That Help You Sing With Ease

Lesson 23: *Legato* As the Pathway To Your Own Beautiful Voice

Something that is helpful to understand is that when we are singing a song and the notes are going up and down our range, because of the way we normally speak, an individual vowel sound, like an E, can actually sound one way in the low or chest register and completely different in the middle or upper head registers. This variation of the quality, and by that, I mean, darker and brighter, varies throughout our vocal registers when our vowels are not consistently felt in the higher, more forward Italianate position.

The problem that is caused by this varying quality, as you can imagine, is that the sound is all over the place. Trying to maintain a smooth or legato sound is almost impossible, if we succumb to the negative attributes of back vowel sounds or diphthongs while we sing. To you and to your listener, it will feel like sometimes the sound is clear and out in front and, at other times, the sound is more swallowed, covered or closed.

For now, we will go back to the vowels, and how knowing where they were being directed in my mouth so dramatically impacted my life as a singer. One day, after studying with Edward for about six to eight months intensively, I was singing through one of my Italian exercises in the shower—I, too, hid while practicing, at least in the beginning! He had asked me to do this one particular exercise, focusing solely on the Italian pure vowel sounds of each syllable and not the words. As you can imagine, it took my mind a moment to adjust to this idea of removing the consonants and singing only vowels. As I did this however, something magical happened! For a brief—and I mean very brief—moment, I felt an unusual smoothness to the sound that I had not yet experienced in the vocal studio.

The next day, I tried again, repeating the same exercise without using any consonants. This time I focused my awareness on keeping one vowel sound consistent throughout the piece. I think that the first one I tried this on was E. Now, every time I came to an E sound in the phrase, I would try to make sure I was singing it in exactly the same spot under my nose, with the same bright Italian quality. I began to notice that each E that I came to was easier and easier to sing.

Eventually I worked my way through all the vowel sounds, bringing my awareness to each AH, each E, each A, each O and each OO in such a way that a consistency of sound started to occur. Remember, of course, that what I was trying to recreate was the Italian vowel placement, so during the exercise I made a point of keeping a tiny mischievous smile on my face with my upper teeth showing, and staying relatively still in the mouth, feeling the vowels directed just below my nose, as opposed to trying to hear them. The more that I became aware of where those vowels were vibrating the more I was able to control them. Keep in mind that I was fighting the urge to let the back vowels return to where they more naturally resonate, towards the back of the mouth.

The day that I was able to maintain consistent forward production of all five vowels was the day I went from being amateur to truly being on the road to professional. For that was the day when not only was the sound incredibly smooth and connected, but the exercise became absolutely effortless to sing. I didn't even feel either of the two passaggios and there was nothing interrupting the sound, even while singing with the consonants.

Once someone asked my teacher why anyone would spend oodles and oodles of money on voice lessons with him and his reply was very simple, if you want to be a professional you have to sing your repertoire the same way over and over again with absolute consistent production. Think of a Broadway performer who sings eight shows a week and you will understand what he was referring to.

So feeling when your voice is working, noticing what you are doing correctly and repeating that behavior over and over again is the practice of getting you to a place where you can be confident that when you open your mouth to sing, you will know exactly what is going to come out. This is very helpful for your preparation should you choose to go out in the world and sing in public!

Lesson 24: How a *Crescendo* Is More Then Just Getting Louder

Once our breath support is stable and sustained, our musculature engaged and lifted, and our vowel sounds unified and forward, how do we maintain this legato or smooth vocal line? The way I would describe legato, which literally means line, has to do with our intentional energy. For those of you that ski, golf, paint, run, or dance, perhaps you can equate this principle with that feeling of balance and control that needs to occur in order to do any of the above consistently and fluidly.

When you ski down a slope, there is a leaning into a curve that gives the skier a sense of connection, both to his or her skis and also to the mountain. A golfer knows that connecting the swing requires a delicate coordination of muscles from the beginning of the swing through contact with the ball, and then the follow-through. Painters feel this feeling when they complete a long, smooth stroke on a canvas. Runners know the concept when they are approaching and taking a hill, even a small one. Dancers, ballerinas, let's say, have to use a certain amount of consistent energy when approaching a lift or jump and, if they don't, the motion will not coordinate and, in a worst-case scenario, they risk injury.

Singers contend with the same kind of energy principle. For example, when I go to sing a high note in a phrase if I do not lift, apply some momentum, pull back on my airflow and add additional air pressure, that note will not want to coordinate properly. I will either not reach it at all, or the approach will tend to be from underneath the pitch and it will most likely sound a bit flat or dull.

So, one way in which I teach this principle is through the concept of a *crescendo*. Literally, in music, a crescendo means that the sound gets louder. But I use the term crescendo more energetically, like leaning into a hill or a swing or a jump. Think about your foot leaning on the accelerator of a car. When you are going up a steep hill, you may feel that steady pressure under your foot that requires you to stay on the pedal until you reach and pass over the top of the hill. Then, the opposite motion becomes important, pulling off of the pedal as you descend the hill on the other side.

This feeling and example is very much akin to the energy I feel when I lean into a phrase in places that require more intensity, and then the gentle pulling back on the energy, so that I don't over-sing the parts that require less. Typically, in a phrase, this would occur as I am approaching and then passing by higher notes, but in truth this kind of leaning in and out happens anywhere we are trying to create a beautiful arc or shape to a phrase.

For me the legato line exists in and of itself, outside of the breath, the support, the notes, the words, the very music itself. Legato is an intentional energy that drives the song from underneath everything else and is very difficult to teach. The easiest way to try and define it physically is through the above more athletic examples. Another possible way to understand the energy is by going back to our kinesthetic learning process.

If we draw a line in the air in front of us, using a limp wrist, you will feel a sort of looseness to the process. Now straighten your hand

and while imagining that you have a piece of saltwater taffy to stretch, make that same line. There is a tension in this second approach that is akin to a physical sensation I feel in my body when I am aware that I am singing with a lot of legato.

It's like an imaginary tension in the air that is literally supporting the entire process of singing, and is something that I am intending to do rather than assuming will happen accidentally. It won't. Not in a million years. Legato is an elusive part of the puzzle and yet, it is the glue that holds an entire song together. When you are listening to a beautiful voice that moves you emotionally, typically you are hearing the legato in that voice.

You'll notice that the singer seems to spin sound effortlessly. Every singer is unique—no two voices are really ever the same—and yet, with all the different possibilities of timbre or color, weight— heaviness or lightness, male or female, beauty can exist in all voices when they share this one element—legato, a smooth and connected sound that never disengages, dulls or drops.

Lesson 25: Developing Vocal Agility: Why It's So Challenging For Some

In the bel canto world, I am called a *Coloratura Soprano*. In my thirties, I was considered a *Lyric Coloratura*, which is a lighter, higher type of singer with a lot of vocal flexibility. These are the operatic sopranos that sound sort of like birds. If I were singing operatic repertoire now, a few years down the road, I would probably be considered more of a *Dramatic Coloratura*, because as voices age they tend to naturally develop more weight. In the world of opera, there are eight different types of sopranos, ranging from the dramatic to the lighter, delicate voices.

The reason I share this with you is that some voices naturally have the ability to move with ease, or what we would call vocal agility.

Other voices, the ones with more weight or a darker timbre to them, typically don't move as easily. In some classical schools of thought, the issue of agility is not addressed for these kinds of voices. They focus on what they do best, beautiful legato lines, smooth and steady.

But in the bel canto training principles, the idea exists that all voices can move quickly no matter what the predisposed weight or timbre. How does this occur in a voice that does not naturally want to move fast?

As with most of the work I do, the clue lies once again in the vowel sound one is choosing. If the vowel chosen is dark and in back, a voice, no matter what type, will have difficulty moving quickly. However, if the vowel we are choosing to phonate is a bright, forward, pure Italian vowel, the vocal agility factor goes up exponentially.

In the vocal studio I was a member of for four years in San Francisco, I was blessed to witness my teacher working with more than 50 voices of all types, both male and female. The process was always the same: narrow and compress or brighten to a forward Italian vowel while maintaining the true integrity of that pure vowel and, if singing a complicated melismatic phrase, constantly refresh the proper vowel sound in the mind throughout. As an example, think of Handel's *Messiah* and all the vocal pyrotechnics in that work.

Compression is similar to being in a recording studio, where a voice is put through a machine that takes out some of the highs and lows. This is done to equalize the sound and make it sound less like it went out of bounds or off course. This compression concept works when we sing too. By creating our nice, round lifted inner amphitheater, we in essence create a balanced acoustic room. When we incorporate both the lifted ceiling and the lowered jaw, we are essentially providing the space for truly balanced sound, with neither too much low resonance nor excessive piercing highs.

So when we stabilize our instrument, sustain our breath, maintain our lovely pure vowels and apply the proper amount of energy, we can maneuver with far greater ease within a line that demands flexibility. This sounds pretty complicated and, in truth, it is to some degree, but it's not unattainable. The integration and the steady energy required to sing these kinds of phrases just require practice. It took me four years of focused attention on the soprano solo parts of Handel's *Messiah* before I ever performed the work in public, but when I did, it was effortless.

Here is one extra tip about learning this kind of complicated music: learn the notes slowly. Our brains require a certain amount of software programming time, and when we are trying to learn complicated patterns in music, the key is to slow the patterns down and learn them in very small sections, even just four or five notes at a time. Once these patterns are consistent in small increments, tie the sections together, one by one.

For those of you that have tried to sing this particular work at Christmas or Easter time, you know the issues I am speaking of. There are patterns in this kind of music where the notes will turn abruptly in a different direction. It is those spots that require extra attention while learning them. If the brain can memorize the turns, it will be able to put the pieces of the musical puzzle together with greater ease and speed up the delivery accordingly.

If you get a chance, I highly recommend attending a *Messiah* performance or listening to a recording of it, for those of you reading this that have never done so. Even if you aren't singing, you will learn a lot from listening to this work, for the vocal agility required to do this type of repertoire is quite amazing to experience.

In a contemporary music context, if you think about singers like Christine Aguilera, Mariah Carey, Ella Fitzgerald and other singers that do what is referred to as scatting, building this vocal flexibility or agility is the foundation for that kind of dynamic vocal movement.

Lesson 26: Anchoring in the Low So That You Can Sing High

As you know, the chest voice is located in the lowest part of your vocal range. The number of notes that are part of this register can vary from person to person, depending on how low you can sing. Some aspects of this part of the voice are tricky to deal with as a singer. So, let's talk about the nature of this section of your instrument and how it impacts the rest of your vocal range.

For most singers, I will begin vocalizing, for women, G below middle C and for men, the same, an octave below. Some singers have additional notes available below the G, but for most sopranos and baritones, this is the starting pitch we use. In some cases, a singer will have difficulty articulating in this part of the voice. Notes will feel awkward to vocalize with ease and, if you are watching yourself in the mirror, you may notice that you will lower your head and have the feeling of trying to sing the note. You may, at this point, feel the sound in your throat. This orientation towards searching for the pitch down here is problematic, as the voice will not easily cooperate with this approach.

As counterintuitive as this is, in order to articulate low notes with more ease, you will need to utilize a higher frontal lift, perhaps show your teeth, add more speech energy into the sound on the attack and keep your rib support steady. I often say the lower you go, the higher you lift.

Because the chest voice is more closely related to speech than the other parts of the vocal range, we need to be even more aware of how we are articulating—fast, crisp and clean—with steady, consistent rib support. This stabilizing support becomes absolutely crucial to your vocal health. The amount of pressure that can inadvertently be put on the voice down here can cause major alignment issues and worse. It is important to take this part of the voice seriously, when it comes to developing good control. For example, there are professionals who use quite a lot of weight in their sound, develop vocal issues associated with fatigue, lack of support and possibly incorrect usage of air, all of which are preventable, and have had to cancel tours due to these challenges.

So, how do we get started working on this area? Let's start by connecting this region of the voice with your speech understanding. If you are able to sit at a piano somewhere, you can prove this speech connection by saying a few words and trying to locate the general pitch you normally speak on. All of us tend to orient our speaking voice around two or three notes, and in general many of us tend to speak too low. Even I, after all these years of vocal work, find myself speaking on tones around G below middle C, when really I should be speaking closer to middle C itself, for my type of voice, in order to take pressure off the vocal cords.

So how do we effectively utilize the chest register in the alignment principles we've been speaking about throughout this book? My bel canto teacher, Edward, always reminded us that we needed to have a strong chest voice in order to sing the higher notes with brilliance. The challenge is that if we push too hard in the chest voice, we will literally push the rest of the voice out of alignment.

Imagine again that the voice is like a pyramid, heavier on the bottom and lighter on the top. As we sing up through our vocal registers, we can feel this shaving off of weight and narrowing of sound, as we do some of our vocal exercises. But, ultimately we need to allow for a little bit of the weight on the very top of our head register and a bit of the lighter quality of the head register on our bottom notes to give them more brilliance. Said another way, we need a tiny amount of low in our highs and a little bit of high in our lows.

This helps create one seamless voice versus two or three different registers with varying qualities.

So as I think about it, as we anchor the foundation, our very lowest notes become like a springboard to get to our top notes. This is accomplished by gently but firmly articulating the lowest notes in our range closer to how we speak with a forward vowel orientation and lift, maintaining the height of the inner smile. By establishing and keeping the inner structure lifted and stable, we are able to navigate up through the first passaggio into the middle register and all the way up to our top notes. For all intents and purposes, this stabilized high structure will enable our voice to modify weight naturally, almost without thought.

If you can vocalize from the G below middle-C through to, say, the F above middle-C without noticing any major shifting through that first passaggio, then your weight-to-support ratio is in good shape. But if you find that the voice feels awkward around C or D, you may have been too aggressive or, in some cases, too loud, on the vocalization of the lowest notes.

Just go back and try again, this time backing off the volume just a touch and see if that doesn't help solve the problem. Be sure to check that your ribcage is energized throughout your vocal exercise and that you are engaged with both your inner smile and frontal lift.

Chapter 9: Troubleshooting

Where Pitch Problems Come From

If your musculature is lifted and engaged and you are still having pitch issues, then we have to look to the mind and the occasional doubt that occurs right before articulation. Just the one stray thought, "Am I singing the right note?" will be enough to send a pitch elsewhere. It really doesn't take much to send a singer off course in this realm.

Sometimes the pitch is dull or appears to be flat, because of the actual vowel placement. Go to the mirror and sing the note again. Notice if you are energized and lifted, or whether you have dropped the lift of the cheeks and inner smile. Forward, bright Italian pure vowels will not be flat or sharp in general.

In the rare instance, pitch will be a totally random and chaotic experience for a singer. I have had two students in fifteen years where this has been the case. One of the gentleman hadn't had music as a part of his life at home as a child. In our world, that seems so unusual, but I believe because of this lack of exposure, he didn't developed the inner listening process that occurs within the brain.

In essence, our brain hears the tone right before we sing it. Our mind sends a very rapid message to the vocal folds or larynx, which in turn creates a pitch. Now remember, that is all the larynx does—it creates a tone, which when combined with articulation, lips, teeth and tongue for the consonants and vowels from the pharynx, we sing a word. So at any one of these stages, the pitch can be affected by a doubting thought, inaccurate tone in the mind or misplaced vowel sound.

Hopeless, You Ask?

If a student has no relationship to pitch, some people will use the term tone deaf. I don't do this. Very few people are actually unable to hear pitch or tones. If you are capable of hearing the phone ring, you are not tone deaf. I believe that even in challenging situations, it is still possible to teach the brain the process of identifying the proper pitch or tone. In the case of one man, it took nine months of lessons to do so. So, I am not saying that it is necessarily easy or fun to go through that kind of relearning; however, it is possible. This gentleman went from singing no accurate pitches to 90 percent accuracy in those nine months.

We did this by sitting side-by-side at a piano, where I would play one note and repeat that note three times, with the student just listening, sometimes with eyes closed. Then I would play it again and ask him to sing the note. If he was above or below the pitch, I would let him know which direction he needed to go to fix it and have him try again. Sometimes there were notes that appeared to be relatively easy for him to get and repeat, as if his hearing was able to be more accurate in these areas. Other spots felt hopeless for a long time. But with patience and diligence, even these areas became more accessible for him within a few months. As a side note, when someone accurately matches a pitch, there is usually a visceral feeling in the body that it is right, so you'll want to tune into how you are feeling in your body during this process. Dissonance, which is caused by two notes that are clashing, also produces (singular rather than plural) a certain feeling of discomfort, both to the ears and to the body. Tuning in to what you are feeling when you sing becomes very helpful for developing consistency.

When we got to a point where this student was able to match fifty percent of the tones, we chose a few songs that were familiar to him as an adult—in his case, from his church repertoire, as he had heard these songs repeated over the past few years. Somewhere in his mind a memory of these songs was stored and as I would play a line of the song on the piano, he was almost immediately able to sing most of the phrase on the right pitch. Again, this still took time, as we would work one phrase on only the melody, until he was comfortable. Once one phrase was consistent, we would build by adding another and so on. Eventually, he was singing songs with his daughter and at church, which had been his original goal.

As you can imagine, this process required enormous patience on both of our parts. But the rule was, no negativity allowed on his part or my part. Just focused, constructive instructions that guided him to finding something that was already there—his voice.

Patient Audio Listening (P.A.L.): Why You Need a Recorder

Two of the key elements to learning how to sing include getting over our fears of looking at ourselves in a mirror and, perhaps even more scary, listening to ourselves on a recording, without judgment. This willingness to listen becomes critical, because for a while, as I mentioned, we may not like how we sound. But if we don't look and listen, we cannot effectively correct our individual issues.

I was watching a David Ledbetter golf coaching video, and he was saying the same thing about golfing and developing a great golf swing: if you are having problems and are unwilling to look at them, you cannot fix them. But if you will not be afraid to look and, perhaps more importantly, not go into judgment mode, you will very quickly be able to discern what is not working.

In the case of my student with the pitch issues, it was important that he have me nearby giving him immediate feedback as to his accuracy. This is one reason why having a compassionate, supportive vocal coach can be so important. We will talk a little later about how to find one of these coaches, but suffice it to say that, in singing, because we can't hear ourselves accurately, we need another pair of ears and/or a recording device that allows us to objectively listen back to ourselves.

I will never forget my teacher stopping me one day, rather upset with me, and saying, "Stop trying to listen to yourself. That is why you are paying me!"

He reminded me that not only could I not hear myself effectively, but that I really needed to start feeling my voice when it worked properly, in order to integrate the new muscular awareness.

He and I always used a recorder in my vocal sessions. I do the same with my students. And it's interesting: the ones that actually spend an hour or two between sessions re-listening to their lesson are the students that move very quickly through their technical work and start to create dramatic results for themselves.

P.A.L.—Patient Audio Listening, means listen to your self without judgment, without worrying about it being perfect, and without creating any new negative beliefs. Just listen. Be the observer. Notice what is working and what is not working. Notice what you like and what you don't like. Be willing to address both.

If you like something about the singing, then identify what parts of our preparation are helping you create that sound, so that you can more effectively integrate and remain aware of them. If there is something you don't like (and for most us, this will be the longer list, at least for a little while), identify what that thing is and see if you can analyze and discover, based on our eight steps, what is not working for you (breathe, lift, engage, maintain, articulate, legato, intention, arc).

One of my students, JoAnn, has only been working with me for a short time. But her enthusiasm for what she is learning is infectious. She has me on the edge of my seat when she bursts into her lessons ready to take on the next technical challenge. JoAnn is willing to commit herself 100 percent to the process, so much so, that I don't mind spending extra time with her working on some small detail that she is having trouble with. She tries everything I ask her to try. Her willingness to be coached is extraordinary, and her commitment to listening back to her lessons and practicing every day, even just for a few minutes, is the driving force behind her amazing results in such a short period of time.

If There Is Pain, There Won't Be Gain or Constriction Is Not Constructive

One of the primary challenges to overcome when we are first learning to sing is the feelings of constriction that can happen at different times. There is no positive purpose to constriction, other than showing us that we are doing something incorrectly. If you are feeling tight in the throat it is not constructive or necessary. I will take it one step further— if you are feeling anything in your throat, it is not correct. There are teaching styles that actually ask you to feel and manipulate your vocal folds or larynx. In my opinion this is not only unnecessary, it is potentially dangerous.

There are certain exercises that I have been trained to do that will stretch the muscles of the throat and exercise the lifting of the soft palate and lowering of the larynx naturally, but none of these exercises requires me to constrict the area. So I make the bold statement that constriction is not constructive, but follow that with the understanding that recognizing when we are constricted can lead us to potential solutions.

Our breath control, maintaining just a small steady stream of air with engaged and energized ribs, takes the responsibility off of the throat to make sound. This act of physical support is the strongest solution and preventative measure we can use for eliminating constriction. For when the body is the foundation for making and sustaining sound, we will feel nothing in our throats.

Sometimes, constriction is literally caused by our mind thinking we don't know what to do. Then, an impulse will occur to push or almost yell to make sound, a forced or pressed kind of feeling. If you have been singing hard-driving music, like rock or heavy metal, this constriction could be the by-product of overuse. Without support of any kind, the harder demands of this kind of music will have our throats work too hard to try and make it all happen. Typically, singers in these genres wear out their voices in a relatively short period of time. This is not irreversible, however, as you remember my student Barbara was able to learn how to support and then return to the music she loved to perform, this time without jeopardizing her voice and career.

Constriction may also be caused by unacknowledged emotional events, like abuse-related issues, which sometimes leave residual physical maladies that interrupt and in some cases, prevent clear, free vocalization. These issues tend to show up when the emotional body is stressed, which can happen in a private voice lesson pretty easily— another reason to make sure you're in a supportive environment when you coach with someone.

I think that taking voice lessons might be one of the most vulnerable things we can do as human beings, especially if we are taking private lessons, or working one-on-one with a coach. Our voice or throat chakra is the place where our personality communicates out into the world. Any known or unknown blockages or emotional issues may prevent singers from doing so with ease, even after they are trained to sing well.

I remember being in my vocal studio in San Francisco and watching fifty professionally aspiring singers working tirelessly with my master teacher, Edward. One night, a tenor stood up and sang a breathtaking aria he had prepared for an upcoming competition. This singer returned to the studio sometime later, only to reveal that he had not done well and felt that he had emotionally sabotaged his audition. I remember my teacher saying that the most technically proficient singers could lose it in a single moment, by one stray negative thought.

So, something like constriction or tightness in the throat while singing is either being caused by an incorrect musculature approach or an emotional issue. That cause needs to be identified and eliminated, either with a coach or on our own.

This again points to the need for you to trust your coach and have the kind of relationship with him or her that allows you to be honest and forthcoming about what you are experiencing, both physically and emotionally.

Sharp Twinge of Pain Means S.T.O.P.

If you ever feel actual pain in your throat while you are singing, something is wrong. Not only is constriction problematic, but also sharp pain should be a warning sign to stop immediately whatever you are doing and identify what is causing the discomfort. First thing to do is check your support and second thing is to check and see if you moved your head and neck abruptly while phonating.

Once while I was exercising my voice, I made the mistake of turning my head sharply to one side. I don't remember if I was interrupted while working the voice or something else occurred, but when I moved I got a cramp in one of the muscles of my throat and it scared me, because it took a minute or so to release.

Sometimes this will happen if you are eating and you turn your head while you swallow. I don't recommend this action, as it causes that same kind of gripped feeling. If you feel pain while you are singing, just remember this: S.T.O.P.!

If you are with your coach and it happens, let her know that it hurts. Something is not being approached properly.

When I sing, I literally feel nothing, other than the gentle, but firm, energy of the tones as they vibrate and leave my mouth. I am thinking like crazy and my brain is definitely working overtime, but I don't feel anything in my throat while I am singing and eventually, with practice, neither will you.

If the Sound Is Too Breathy

While you are singing a phrase, if you notice that there is a breathy quality to the sound, it can normally be attributed to two things: either there is a tendency to insert an H, right as the articulation process happens or there is a general lack of breath control, where it feels like the body is over-releasing or pressing air out while you are singing. You may notice that when you breathe, your ribs immediately begin to collapse, thus pressing air out like a bellows.

If you record yourself, you will hear the H if it is present and you will feel excess air pressure on the attack. For the record, there are certain classical orientations that specifically use an H at the beginning of articulation, as it can create the experience of a softer approach to the initial sound. This can be seen as desirable in certain types of classical music. Choral directors often like to use this approach for easier blending of attacks as it will soften a group's overall articulation.

In bel canto we are avoiding excess air in the sound, so that initial attacks stabilize the vocal mechanism in a more quick and effective way, thus making the process easier on the singer to control their legato line. The softening of the initial attack is done with a gentle articulation that is controlled within the mind, as it artistically designs the arc of the phrase. In other words, adding extra air is not necessary to create the desired effect, even in a choral setting, but the amount of time required to get every singer at the same level of vocal technique becomes the challenge.

If you listen to really good singing groups however, like Westminster Chorus or the King's Singers, you will hear a more controlled articulation style that rarely uses air as the mechanism to get the artistic result.

If you are singing Broadway music or any style where you want to be able to create clear diction, the airy approach is not effective. In essence, by pushing a large quantity of air through the mechanism on articulation, we are almost pressing the vocal cords open while we are trying to bring them together to stabilize. So, moving toward producing a gentle, yet precise, crisp consonant or vowel at the beginning of a phrase quickly coordinates the vocal mechanism and creates stability in the sound, while increasing your capacity to control your singing. This is akin to getting on that little railroad track and maintaining a constant feeling in the Buzz area below the nose that allows us to stay on that line throughout the entire phrase.

If your articulation is fine, but you are still noticing a breathy overall quality to the sound, you may want to go back and do the breath control exercise on the floor every day for a couple of weeks or so. Reorienting the body to understanding that it needs only a small amount of air to make sound will help integrate this principle while you are singing.

A trick I sometimes use to help a student get things stabilized quickly is to imagine that when you breathe in, you are going to hold your breath for a second as you articulate. The reality is that as soon as you make sound, the small stream of breath will be moving. But this split second of not consciously releasing the air as you articulate helps stabilize the mechanism and often you will notice a clearer, less breathy phrase immediately. Imagine if you will, that our job is to get the vocal cords stabilized and vibrating with the air behind them, quickly establishing a steady air pressure. I feel an almost constant sensation of holding energy back throughout my phrases.

With voices that are more mature, or are out of control completely, I will have the student focus on not releasing excess air and working hard to not collapse the ribs. Sometimes by holding the air back completely, a student will experience free, effortless sound and, even though it is incredibly counterintuitive, less air helps everything coordinate more easily.

So, although a small amount of air is really moving through the instrument, once we begin articulation, my inclination is never to push air through, but rather just allow the musculature to control that by focusing on sustaining the open ribs, which maintains steady gentle air pressure necessary to keep control of the breath. The only exception to this is when dealing with certain high notes, at which point I do become conscious of lifting my inner smile higher and increasing the gentle air pressure through momentum, by leaning into the rib support even more.

If the Sound is Nasal

Typically, a nasal sound is caused by a collapsed soft palate and can be rectified by the inner smile. To be honest, this doesn't happen too often in my vocal studio, because of the way I address the frontal lift and directed articulation. However, I know that it can be a problem for some singers. As I understand it, when the soft palate is dropped in the back, if a lot of air is flowing through the mechanism, that air can be inadvertently directed up into the back of the sinuses, which causes that honking sensation in the nose area.

The French language nasal sounds are actually supported with that lowered and relaxed soft palate, but in most contemporary American music, we are not looking for that type of sound quality.

So, remember, the Buzz area is just below the nose, not in it or above it. Sometimes, just by directing a singer to aim lower in their articulation energy, the nasal issue can be solved. But, in most cases, we need to address the lifting of the inner smile as the solution to that problem and focus our attention again on controlling our exhalation, not pressing air up into the mouth.

If a High Note Won't Work

As mentioned above, high notes may require more momentum to resonate and ring properly. Remember, our inner smile and lifted soft palate need to be very high in order to create enough space for these notes to sing. This height is established on the initial breath preparation, as we inhale into that lifted position, essentially breathing and preparing for the highest note in any given phrase each time. Maintaining additional space between the molars, or creating that Jimmy Stewart feeling in the mouth, also aids resonance, as it creates more ease in this part of the vocal range.

So there are a few pieces to the puzzle when we are dealing with this particular issue. What I normally suggest as I am walking a student through this challenge is to remember to prep the breath, lifting the soft palate to the highest position necessary for the phrase, at the beginning of the phrase, trying not to wait until the last moment, as it then becomes difficult to quickly adjust the musculature, and this lack of preparation will lead to scooping or slurring into notes.

Once the musculature is in proper position, articulate crisply, but gently, on the first word of the phrase, and then, as you are approaching the difficult note, start to lean in, as if putting a bit more pressure on your gas pedal, and give the phrase a bit more energetic momentum as you are going up, over and through the highest notes. When we are accustomed to control our air in a small steady stream, this process will almost feel like I am pulling back the air and increasing pressure at the same time. It is an odd counter motion that is almost like the bow and arrow feeling.

It is like I am pulling back energetically and the sound is going forward, but the amount of air I'm feeling go through the mechanism remains the same. I have to admit that this is an odd feeling. For we almost immediately want to push air and increase volume when we go for these high notes, but if we don't, something amazing happens. The high notes are actually more effortless to coordinate. I will literally force myself to not change dynamic levels as I go higher. To feel the ease I speak of requires trust, lots of space and height inside the mouth and very forward vowels located in the same Buzz spot, like that one condo, one floor image. Kinesthetically, we can sometimes assist ourselves by moving an arm in the motion of going up and over a roller coaster or around a Ferris wheel, being careful not to push extra air.

Sometimes, when high notes fall in our second passaggio area, our bodies will really start to push and when this occurs, we almost always drop our lifts. This is caused by that counterintuitive quality we spoke about in the beginning of the book. The body thinks that if it pushes the sound it will work better when, in truth, the opposite is true.

By not forcing too much air through the vocal folds, we keep them stabilized and oscillating together, and often we will find that we phonate high notes with greater ease.

Keep in mind that singing high notes beautifully is one of the most challenging technical aspects of singing, and it takes patience to integrate and time to establish consistency. Repeating one difficult phrase over and over again, reinforcing the proper approach, will anchor and stabilize the sound as well as help develop consistency. Just remember to slow down and really prepare, both your breath and your mind. This will help you also analyze what is not quite working, as you repeat the passage.

Practice, practice, practice is key.

If You Run Out of Air Too Soon

Sometimes while we are singing a song, a phrase will sneak up on us and we will realize way too late that we don't have enough breath to handle the sentence. We can go back to the practice of making sure that we are not letting too much air slip away at the beginning of the phrase. For example, if the sentence is structured in an easy part of the vocal range to begin with and then moves into a more difficult area, like the passaggio, we want to try and remember that we are going to need more gas to get up and over that section. So it becomes about breath management at this point.

If your sound is too breathy, go back to the breathing exercises for a while to assist your body to integrate the control factor. But if that is not the case and you are still having difficulty getting enough air to last the whole sentence, then I recommend a couple of things.

We often need to analyze our song from start to finish, in terms of where the problems are going to challenge us. In this case, we are looking for those spots where the composer has created longer than usual phrases for us to sing. Once identified, we want to take those individual phrases and work them by themselves for a while. I always start by singing the sentence on the Italian sound NI (nee) and will work that one area until I can make it through the entire phrase on one breath.

This establishes the core line, as well as teaches the vocal mechanism how to maneuver through the arc of the sentence, indicating where the breath wants to give out, and how much control we will need to manage it. Once I can sing the phrase on NI effectively, I will then add the real words back in, watching out for any pitfalls.

One specific pitfall that can occur with this kind of breath-related challenge is the H sound. Double-check and make sure that you are not articulating H's before any words that you are singing. They tend to sneak in when we are singing a word that starts with a vowel and also can happen when a composer gives us a syllable that is sung over several moving notes. Often, we will find that we inadvertently place H in front of each note, as we move. If that happens, just remember to refresh or more clearly articulate the actual vowel sound you are on with each new note.

Once again, when I am breathing, I am thinking that I am becoming the tank of air, not just filling the tank with air. After the ribs are engaged, I am consciously holding back releasing air, maintaining a sense of air pressure in my ribcage. If you exhale and then inhale and hold your breath, you will feel a pressure in your chest. This pressure, when maintained while singing, sustains our phrases, even our long ones. Less, not more, air is the solution for vocal challenges and sentences that seem too long to sing.

Don't be surprised if suddenly you have tons of air left over. Just remember to inhale into that lifted amphitheater in your mouth and re-engage the ribs each time you breathe. If we never drop our energy or heightened state of being while singing, we can go through an entire song with more accuracy, effectiveness and control.

Just be sure that when you first inhale that you are expanding your ribs horizontally and maintaining that position throughout your phrase. Allowing the ribs to collapse will automatically force air out of the instrument. So, once you have determined that you are articulating properly, check your ribs on these difficult passages.

If Your Pitch Becomes Flat

As we have discussed in our earlier lessons, this particular pitch issue is normally caused by vowel placement and speech-related dropping of the ends of syllables, and is rectified by using the forward, brighter Italian pure vowel. The challenge, of course, is caused by the fact that we might not be Italian, and some of what we are practicing feels very counter to our normal speech habits. (On a side note, those who do have Italian ancestry often find the principles I work with easier to execute. Something seems to translate in the DNA; so, if you are fortunate enough to have those genes, don't hesitate to feel animated!)

When we are trying to identify which specific vowels are causing us problems, typically it is our back sounds— AH, O, U, and don't forget the schwa, UH— that are the culprits. We will need to go back to the mirror first and look to see if we are being consistent with our forward lift on those sounds. There is a propensity to drop our cheeks and mouths automatically on certain words and, if this action is causing a pitch to go flat, once it is stabilized you should feel the tuning improve.

If we are lifted and the pitch is still problematic, then the next place to look at is our energy. If a syllable or sound is not given enough energy to stay aloft, the pitch will suffer. Make sure that as you are singing, you are not only energizing your vocal mechanism, but you are energizing your intention and thoughts. Imagine being around someone who is excited about something that has just happened—that is the kind of energy we need when we sing.

If Your Pitch Is Sharp

Pitch that tends to go sharp is rare and in my experience mostly caused by stress and worry. Typically a singer is trying so hard to do everything correctly that they press on the voice just a bit too hard and the sound gets shifted to a slightly more strident place. I have only experienced this challenge with a few students over the years. One of the students tended to go sharp in performance, and this was clearly related to the nerves associated with other aspects of singing, as she never manifested the issue in the vocal studio.

Another was someone who struggled with early pitch training and tended to go both flat and sharp. This appeared to me to be more about the mind trying to figure out how to make a pitch, versus a problem with phonating a tone. We addressed this issue with both Patient Audio Listening and vocalizing work at the piano, and the use of a recording device, to help this student discover the challenge.

In the rare case of someone dropping his or her forward lift and letting their voice recede into their mouth, they will start pushing to recover, especially on high notes. When this kind of in-and-out singing gets intense, there can be the tendency to push to get up to the top notes of the vocal range and you will literally push them up too high. Maintaining the forward lift, focusing on maintaining steady breath control, and not trying so hard can often ease this situation.

Pulling back and singing with a lighter quality may assist you in getting a handle on this kind of pressure issue. Sometimes I will put my hand up in front of my face about six inches away and sing only to my hand. This typically prevents me from pushing too hard on the sound.

Of course, no one wants to sing flat or sharp, so if this is a challenge for you, please try to remember that the core issue is not personal, but has to do with the actual approach to the sound and the stabilization of your musculature. Return to the earlier lessons on how to lift, think about your vowels and retraining the mind to think thoughts that benefit your sound. These sections will help you work through the challenge without creating another negative belief system about the voice.

If It Feels Like the Sound Is Collapsing

When we are in the middle of sustaining a note in a phrase, occasionally we will feel like we lose control and there is an overall drop in both the pitch and the energy of the sound. This is often caused by the diphthong and the pitfall of succumbing to the sagging associated with our language issues. Keep in mind that, especially for us as Americans, every single syllable wants to close down and become a two-part sound, even if it is not a diphthong.

Compounding this challenge in our American approach to the language, we also tend to inflect down at the end of our sentences when we speak. Combine that with the natural tendency to collapse our support right before the end of the phrase, sort of like our minds think we are done two seconds before the end of the sentence and we release our energy, causing the phrase to fall. This energy drop causes an automatic loss of pitch at the end of each phrase.

If we are not conscious of this tendency, we will not even notice it until we listen to a recording and are unhappy with something about the ends of our sentences. This inflecting down also leads to something I call our signature. When we go to finish a phrase, sometimes if you listen carefully, you will hear a pattern of movement that once completed sounds like a little swirly pattern that will then drop.

Most singers have patterns that they will use to finish a note at the end of a phrase; this is our way of signing our sound. The challenge comes from the habitual nature of this unconscious pattern. We don't just do it once—if we are doing it, we do it all the time and every phrase ends with the same energy or drop, as well as this interesting little swirl of sound.

The solution to these challenges is to become aware of how you feel when you sustain a note or finish a sentence, analyze what you sound like, and then try to do what a European would do and at the end of phrases, lift or inflect up, while cleanly releasing the sound. This energetic, intentional inflection in the opposite direction not only stabilizes the sound, but will also help us from going flat at the end of our sustained words and phrases.

In general, we need to realize that it takes intentional energy to sustain our sound. We don't need to press or force it, but there is a feeling of not letting the note value go too soon. This energy is connected to our conversation about the legato line and how we maintain control throughout a phrase. If we remember to connect our speech to our singing, we can use our artistic image of how we would say a phrase, like a poet or actor would read a line with intensity or meaning, and help ourselves to deliver well inflected and articulated phrases when we sing.

If You Have Difficulty Getting a Phrase To Work Consistently

In every song that I have ever learned, there are typically at least two spots that land right in the second or upper passaggio that generate great challenges. Composers and arrangers may not be trained singers and aren't always aware of the vowel-related issues associated with managing and maneuvering through these passageways. Sometimes word placement in a melody line cannot be avoided.

As a result, it falls on the singer to address the issue through understanding the challenges caused by the back vowels, work the phrases with a concentrated core sound, line it up, and train the voice to find the aligned pathway through these areas. This is a time-intensive endeavor, and requires a great deal of patience as the voice will not want to cooperate in the passaggio, particularly on the schwa sound.

If we break these problematic phrases down and practice them on a small bright Italian NI (nee) combined with a lifted inner smile, we will find that eventually the voice finds the little train track we have spoken of previously and will move through the section more easily. I learn all new pieces of music this way, and will actually sing the entire song on NI for several runs, until I feel the pathway the voice needs to follow. Once the legato line is identified and integrated on this small sound, I put the words back in, remembering to identify the problem sounds of: R, L, Uh and Aaaagh.

At this point, as if I were programming software, my voice will understand how to navigate through the passages and makes the necessary adjustments without the mind having to agonize over it. It's almost as if I have preprogrammed the musculature to accommodate the difficulty I will be asked to navigate. As long as we have awareness as to where these challenges occur and prepare for them with things like the forward and inner lifts, we can go to the next step of modifying the problem words and, *voila*, the phrase works better. At this stage of our vocal development, we want to be sure that the lift and support elements are consistent, in order to assist ourselves with the overall vocal approach. In making sure the musculature is stabilized, we can now focus on singing with artistic interpretation.

If You Have Too Much Phlegm

"Phlegm is your friend," said Edward. I remember looking at him like he was crazy and thinking how can that possibly be the case. As he explained to me that day, our voices won't work at all without some mucus. It is a lubrication that is necessary to the process.

I discovered that truth in a rather uncomfortable way. I was in Austria participating in a two-month operatic program and was asked to audition for the faculty upon arrival. Air conditioning in the concert hall where I was singing caused the environment to be very dry. I stepped out on stage and began singing an *aria*. As I approached the end of the song, I noticed that I was feeling like I had cotton in my mouth. Suddenly in the middle of the piece, nothing came out. I couldn't sing a note. As you can imagine, this was not optimal under the circumstances. But by that time it was too late and there was no way to recover. On a side note, biting your tongue gently on the sides does stimulate saliva production and can sometimes assist in these situations.

So when we think about phlegm, it is good to remember that it will always be about management. Too much mucus does get problematic, but none is devastating. The warm-ups that I do include a phlegm-clearing exercise. This exercise shakes off the residual phlegm that may be on the vocal cords from post-nasal drip or allergy related issues, stimulates the sinuses to have them drain any additional mucus so that it is cleared a bit, and then helps the voice line-up the legato in a way that focuses the voice on the core line.

An additional piece of the phlegm puzzle includes not eating or drinking dairy right before you sing and, remember that if you do eat a lot of dairy products, you may find yourself needing to clear the excess phlegm each time you warm-up. I don't normally recommend using lemon to strip phlegm from the throat. In my experience, it is too acidic. Always having water handy is a good idea, as that can help move the excess mucus, once we have started vocalizing.

There are times where environmental things will cause the throat to clog up, sort of like the body's way of trying to compensate for the climate by adding moisture to the instrument. Ultimately, even in these conditions, we can sing through phlegm when we are vocally aligned and use enough energy. Suffice it to say that phlegm management is a bit of an adventure and as you grow as a singer, you will find ways to sing around and through it. With additional support energy, while using the forward lift to bypass feeling anything in the throat while narrowing of the sound, we can circumnavigate the challenge through the use of our bright, pure vowels.

Coughing, Clearing, Yelling, Whispering, Smoking and Alcohol Consumption

All of the above are unhealthy for a singer. Some singers and teachers would add caffeine to the list, as well. Let's address the physical issues first and then we will go to the consumption-related ones.

Coughing and clearing the throat should be avoided whenever possible. If you do get a bad cough, you will want to speak to your doctor about which cough suppressant is best for you to use. Sometimes we need to clear mucus from the lungs and so an expectorant is desirable, but there are cough syrups that have both. This makes the cough more productive and hopefully less frequent. Clearing the throat is very common for us to do, especially if we are dealing with phlegm-related challenges, but it is not ideal for the vocal cords. Imagine that both coughing and clearing are akin to smacking or clapping the cords together, and can be very abrasive.

In the extreme, extended coughing can actually cause vocal nodules to form on the larynx. These are raised areas on the vocal folds that prevent them from coming together completely and oscillating properly. A node will cause a gap to occur that allows air to escape constantly. This is why someone with a nodule will sound raspy.

Although surgery is an option to remove them, it is a risky one. Julie Andrews is an example of this surgery going wrong. She lost her ability to sing for some time and, when her voice did return, her range was somewhat limited. I remember crying the day I heard the news of the failed surgery on one of the most beautiful voices of our time. Since then, she has recovered more and more of her ability to sing, but the instrument is not the same as it was prior to the nodules developing.

Truly, nodules and/or polyps are not something we ever want to deal with as singers, and the only way to really insure against their development is through proper support, lifted, engaged singing, and maintaining our vocal health—and even these are not always a guarantee that problems won't arise. If in doubt, go see an ear, nose and throat (ENT) specialist, who can look at the vocal cords to determine what is causing the issue.

Now, yelling can cause the same physical maladies. Kids do it all the time, and sometimes even when they sing, they yell. This is really not healthy for their voices and, if they want to sing, I highly recommend finding a good coach that is willing to work with children on good vocal habits. Unfortunately in the singing world, sometimes these coaches are hard to find. As a parent, just be aware that heavy pressure on the vocal cords can be damaging. All of the principles that we use in bel canto are good for the young voice. Teaching them proper support and vowel placement can alleviate problems and give them a very good head start on vocal development.

On the flip side of the coin, whispering is equally problematic. Too much airflow through the vocal cords is much like sandpaper to them and the friction can also contribute to laryngeal problems. One of the things an ENT doctor will often do for someone suffering from these conditions is to suggest that they do some work with a good vocal coach and/or speech therapist, and breath control and support become tantamount to the healing process.

I am always amazed when singers say to me that they smoke. Some do and some get away with it, seemingly without injury. But, for most of us, that wouldn't be the case. The primary problem with smoking for a singer is dehydration. The vocal cords lose their moisture from exposure to the smoke. A raspy quality to the vocal sound can occur over prolonged use and nodules can develop. These challenges can also occur in a secondary smoke environment, so being aware of how you are physically feeling in the throat can help ward off trouble.

Alcohol also has the same dehydrating properties of smoking. I admit, I like an occasional glass of red wine and so do a number of famous opera singers. In the case of alcohol, moderation seems to be key. Caffeine is also in this category. It can be drying and if someone has a predisposition towards laryngeal reflux, caffeine and wine can exacerbate it.

In general, anything you can do to promote good vocal health will extend your singing life. This includes staying hydrated, getting enough rest and maintaining your voice through good technical understanding.

If You Have Asthma

If you have asthma or allergy-related breathing issues, a side benefit of all the hard work around developing good breath control is that you may find you breathe easier all the time. When you are practicing your breathing exercises, just remember to be gentle with yourself and take them slowly. The breathing aspect of singing for an asthmatic is a challenge in and of itself, but I believe that the act of singing helps the condition.

Learning to control the exhalation through energized and sustained rib pressure means that you use less air. The panic that can occur with asthma can be handled by knowing that you will never run out of air on a phrase. So, as an asthmatic, spending some extra time on this aspect of your vocal development will pay big dividends for you in particular, for with your heightened awareness of how the breathing process affects your singing, once you have established control through the support mechanism, the confidence gained with tend to also permeate your day-to-day life.

Chapter 9: Troubleshooting

When in the vocal studio, there may be occasional moments where you need to let your coach know that you are having difficulties with the breathing, so that he can be more sensitive to your challenges with the process. But the asthmatic singers, whom have studied with me, after a few months, have all said the same thing: "Singing with bel canto understanding has made my overall breathing easier."

Chapter 10: Joining a Choir or Preparing To Audition

What About Practice...How Long Is Too Long?

One summer I took a vocal workshop with Ellen Faull, one of Sarah Brightman's voice teachers at the time, in Portland, Oregon. It was there that I met a coach who was a prompter at the Metropolitan Opera in New York. A prompter is someone who is unseen by the audience, but if you have ever watched a PBS opera production from the Met on television, you may have noticed a little box on the downstage center point of the stage. Inside that box stands a person who cues the performers for each entrance they have to make.

This woman informed us that our practice time each day should never exceed the cumulative performance requirements in any opera, so I have always used the time frame of one hour as the standard.

Some students will find themselves, after a 3-hour choir rehearsal, exhausted and vocally fatigued. This fatigue generally occurs because our ability to effectively support becomes challenged after a certain amount of time, and once the support is gone, all the responsibility for making sound falls on the throat.

Normally a choir rehearsal does not require you to be singing non-stop for those three hours, but you should keep in mind that pacing yourself is a good idea, and that the more that the principles of proper breath preparation, lift and support are in place, the less tiring these longer singing stints are going to be.

Keep in mind that some of the principles of bel canto go against standard vocal practice in the choral environment. Not all choir directors are trained singers and, even if they are, it is likely that they are trained in a more standard operatic fashion, moving a lot of air and using what is affectionately known as belly breathing. This orientation of the breath, from a bel canto standpoint, drops air into the body without engaging the ribs. I have found that singers actually take in too much air, without having a mechanism to control it. In general our approach to air control uses less air with more consistency, making the overall experience of singing more effortless.

But, keep in mind that bel canto produced a very specific type of opera singer: one that maintained absolute control of the legato line, air and core-connected sound. Once opera composers such as Puccini, Verdi and Wagner started producing heavier and more powerful demands on the singer, the breathing process became more demanding as well. This is why it takes opera singers so long to become professionals. They must learn to manage a far greater quantity of air and pressure in order to produce a more powerful, continuous sound.

Contemporary singers do not require the same kind of air movement and, in fact, will have difficulty singing the various genres like jazz, standards, Broadway, pop, alternative and rock with the kind of air approach heavy opera singers require. The specific air management of bel canto with the incorporated ribs is the perfect solution for today's singer, allowing for clear diction and total control of your well-tuned legato line.

You want to be aware that as beautiful as choral music can be, the specific vowel production used can sometimes cause challenges for the singer, due to the director's primary agenda—blend. A darker or farther back orientation to the vowel is often seen as more easily handled in a group setting. This is achieved by orienting the sound farther back in the mouth, rounding the lips with very relaxed dropped lower jaw. The singer's need to be comfortable throughout their vocal range and vocally stress-free is not necessarily always a priority under these circumstances.

In the bel canto work, by creating a stronger more stable instrument, you become the round space that creates that desirable sound, as opposed to manipulating the sound into a darker space with your mouth shape or dropped musculature. My hope is that you will get your instrument in a supported, round, lifted place and be able to maintain your vocal integrity, while accommodating the needs of the choral sound for your director.

As a side note, the discussion in choral circles around the idea of chiaroscuro (light/dark singing), created by the lifted inner instrument and forward vowels, is getting quite a bit of attention and traction. It is my hope in writing this book that directors will get an opportunity to understand what singers are contending with as they work to produce effortless, free, supported sound. Any sound they desire can be created by a well-functioning voice, allowing the mind to artistically design and articulate the sound through a resonant space.

Basics You Need To Know About Reading Music

Most beginners who come to me have some misunderstanding surrounding what it means to read music and often are overwhelmed and discouraged by their lack of ability to do so, especially when they are contemplating joining a choir. So I would like to shed some light on this subject, especially as you are preparing to go out into the world to sing.

Reading music means just that. To read a piece music means that you can identify what you are looking at when confronted with a piece of sheet music. For example, it is helpful to know what a quarter note, half note, eighth note, dotted note, whole note and the equivalent rests look like.

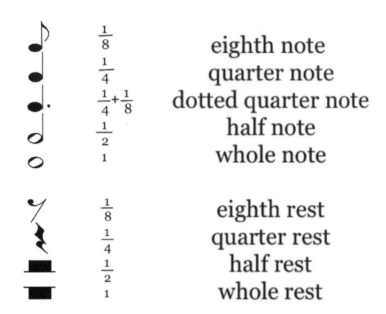

♪	$\frac{1}{8}$	eighth note
♩	$\frac{1}{4}$	quarter note
♩.	$\frac{1}{4}+\frac{1}{8}$	dotted quarter note
♩	$\frac{1}{2}$	half note
o	1	whole note
	$\frac{1}{8}$	eighth rest
	$\frac{1}{4}$	quarter rest
	$\frac{1}{2}$	half rest
	1	whole rest

Measures basically contain an amount of time and are mathematical, for example 4/4 time indicates that there are four quarter notes to a measure. But, those measures can look different when four quarter notes becomes two half notes or a single whole note or eight eighth notes.

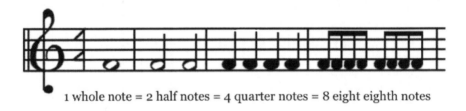

1 whole note = 2 half notes = 4 quarter notes = 8 eight eighth notes

Men and women have to learn to read two different staffs, which are the five lines and four spaces where your notes are written. Women are typically singing in what we call the Treble clef or G-clef, indicated by the little end tail swirl that clef makes around the note G. Most of the time, men read and sing in what we call the Bass clef or F-clef, indicated by the two dots that surround the note F on that staff. In some choral music, however, male tenors will read the treble clef, singing one octave down.

= treble clef (G clef) = bass clef (F clef)

What is kind of weird or difficult to get into mind initially, because of the apparent larger space between the staffs, is that there are only four notes between the top line of the bottom staff and the first line of the top one—B, C, C# (Db) and D. When you look at the pair of staffs, one above the other, note that the F-clef (Bass) is the one on the bottom and the G-clef (Treble) is the one on the top in any given piece of piano vocal music. (When these two staffs are combined, say in a piano arrangement, this is referred to as a system.)

Once you know these basic pieces, you are essentially reading music. It is a misnomer to believe that reading music means you can look at a note and sing it. This particular skill is actually called sight singing, which we will talk about in our next section. Not everyone can do this, and the folks I know who do it effectively and seemingly without effort have been pianists all their lives, or have studied music extensively. As a side note, I don't consider myself a great sight-singer, even after singing for over thirty years, because I am not asked to do it very often. This skill takes focus and improves over time with diligent attention.

I have come to realize that new students can get intimidated at the thought of reading music or sight singing. Just know that the technical aspects of music and music theory are all pieces that can be learned with a little patience and some time. Finding a simple music theory book online, or going to your local music store and asking about classes they might offer, will get you started. Once you have a little information about this aspect of the process, you will feel much more comfortable engaging in singing out in the world.

How Do I Learn To Sight-Sing?

Sight-singing is the ability to look at the notes on a piece of music and, without any assistance from a piano or other instrument, sing those notes. This is predominantly a learned skill. Very few singers or musicians have what is called perfect pitch, the ability to identify and sing an accurate note by looking at it on the page. Most singers have what is called relative perfect pitch, if they have it at all, and that is the ability to be given a note and sing the song while remaining in the proper key, without assistance from an instrument.

As we have been learning, even the ability to hold onto the tonal center or key throughout a song, for us as Americans, is somewhat determined by our ability to prevent the natural speech challenges from coming into play.

So, sight-reading is more likely to be something you would learn in a choir setting over time, by patient diligence on yours and the director's part. Sometimes singers are given a piece of music with their vocal lines and while the piano is playing the accompaniment, the choir sings their melody or harmony lines without being given their individual specific notes. This skill takes time to develop for everyone, and is not something that you should feel threatened by. Just be patient and listen; it will get easier.

One way to start to strengthen your skill level is to understand and hear the relationship between various interval patterns, or distance between two notes, for example, thirds, fourths and fifths. I work with the Vaccai, a series of Italian exercises used in many classical voice traditions that focus on the Italian language. This tool teaches the various note patterns required to read and sing songs with visual ease, as well as offers exercises in ornamentation for classical singing. There are other methods to build sight-singing skills, like *Solfeggio*, often used in larger choir settings, which you may know as the "Do-Re-Mi" approach.

Many beginning and intermediate singers also get a bit intimidated by the demands of understanding music theory. I would say this: there are plenty of singers who don't read music and still do very well. However, for purposes of ease and the mind feeling more comfortable, understanding the basics will help a singer feel more certain about their skills, especially in a choral or group setting.

How Come the Guys Get a Falsetto and the Girls Don't?

We have spoken about how men start vocalizing an octave below a woman's vocal range, but what we haven't touched on yet is how they actually can match us in our head register with something called their falsetto.

A normal healthy range, for both men and women, is approximately two to two and a half octaves. But mysteriously, men are able to continue beyond their normal chest, middle and head registers and take their voices up into another octave into this fourth registration.

For those of you that haven't heard a man sing in falsetto, you might want to check out a recording of *Carmena Burana* by the composer Orff. The monk character in this work sings a significant amount of his repertoire in his falsetto. The sound has a haunting feeling about it and almost mimics a woman's voice, although you can tell it isn't exactly a woman singing.

Now, every man has a falsetto, and how they get there, if you ask them, is often not quite clear to them. It is as if they can flip into this place in their voices such that it almost feels like a detached sound, not connected to the rest of their vocal range.

However, in the bel canto work that I have done and witnessed in my San Francisco studio, there is a belief that the transition between the head and falsetto can be maneuvered through in such a way that the singer doesn't feel such a dramatic shift. It is done with the work of our soft palate and forward lifts, weight balance, as well as the narrowing and compressing of the vowel sounds as the voice moves up through the head register.

I have found that by men strengthening their second passaggio, they allow for more ease going into both the head and falsetto areas of the voice, often delaying the need to move out of the legitimate head register into falsetto. This potentially adds even more notes to one's high end. It is also helpful to work the descending line from the top of the falsetto back into the legitimate head and middle register. If the height of the soft palate required for the very top notes is maintained through that movement, a singer will discover that they can control the transition back into these parts of the voice with more ease. For men that are predominantly singing in their falsetto or head register, I often suggest that they maintain the highest inner smile position they can throughout their singing range. This prevents the weight from automatically dropping into their singing sound when they go below their second passaggio and allows them to return to their falsetto with more ease.

The bel canto work supports the concept of one voice from bottom to top and back down again, so as you can imagine, with all of the little pieces of the puzzle, this aspect of connecting the registers seamlessly takes some time and patience. Keeping the inner smile and forward lift becomes critical to the process. Just know that it is normal for the body to want to drop all the internal musculature, as soon as it starts descending. But, this will add too much weight to the sound too soon and we will lose the ability to control our voice through the transitions.

In order to experience one smooth, connected sound from bottom to top and top to bottom, we must remain engaged in exactly the same way, in both directions. This idea—that our control is maintained in the same way at all times—is the beauty of bel canto. However, the energy required to keep our voices in the zone can sometimes be a bit daunting. Just remember that ultimately it will take less energy to remain engaged then it will to droop and drop continually!

Women traditionally do not have this fourth register or falsetto area in their voices. In the Hawaiian musical tradition, there is a something called a female falsetto that creates an unusual sound that is somewhat detached and is a distinctly different sound from the traditional vocal registers, but it is more a quality of sound than an addition of higher notes.

Amy Hana'iali'i Gilliom is a well-known contemporary Hawaiian singer who uses this technique, as she learned from her Aunty Genoa Keawe, and there are several recordings of Amy's available that you can listen to in order to get a sense of this haunting and beautiful sound.

Finding Your Best Audition Songs

Sometimes when you are interested in joining a choir or performing in a local community theater production, you will be asked to audition. In preparation, the first thing to do is ask the people in charge of the auditions what they would like you to sing. Occasionally, they will say, choose whatever is comfortable for you. Often for a musical, the director will expect you to choose a song that is from another show, not from the production they are casting, but one that shows off your voice well, either up-tempo or ballad and sometimes they will want samples of both tempos.

My sense is the tradition of not auditioning with a song from the actual musical comes from the fact that the director normally has an idea or image of what he or she is looking for in the casting of each role and by singing something from the show itself, it limits that process a bit. So unless they specifically ask for something from the show they are casting, choose from another musical's songs.

If you know what role you are auditioning for, you can try to choose songs from characters that are similar in nature. This is one way you can show off how you would fit into the particular role that you might be interested in performing.

When picking a song for yourself, you want to keep in mind that auditions are very uncomfortable for most people. I have no trouble walking out on stage to perform for a thousand people, but when I have to audition for someone, I become a bundle of nerves. I think it has to do with the subtle communication that we are in a situation where we are to be judged, and whenever we become self-conscious, it is easy to get caught up in our fears of that evaluation process.

So having said that, my best advice is to pick something easy for you to sing that shows off as much of your range as you are genuinely comfortable with, and keep in mind that the accompaniment for the music should also be relatively simple, as you will not always know the level of skill that your pianist will have. One example of a bad choice on my part was the time I decided to sing "The Lonely Goatherd" from *The Sound of Music.*

Now, the song itself is simple enough in its melodic structure and I thought it was the perfect up-tempo choice for a role that I was interested in. However, the tempo I take with this song is really speedy and the tempo my accompanist could handle was not quick at all. The first verse was a disaster and I kept going. (Always important to note: keep going, and try not to look distressed, even if you are completely distracted by something else that is going on. Even though the director will be well aware of the challenges you are facing under these circumstances, he or she will take note of the fact that you were able to handle the situation with poise, under a great deal of pressure.)

In this particular instance, I made a choice to leave my accompanist in the dust and go at my tempo, letting them catch whatever chords or notes they could. But this is not optimal. As much as possible, you want to build a relationship with everyone you meet at your audition. Just as in any other social situation, you never know when that person is going to be making decisions that involve you. So, offending the accompanist is never recommended. Always be very polite, as they control the situation while you are singing.

When you first go into an audition, introduce yourself when it is your turn by saying something like, "Hi, my name is _____ and I would like to sing _____ for you today." If you were asked to prepare two songs, indicate both at this time and either the audition staff will let you choose which one you will start with, or they will let you know which one they want to hear first.

At some point, either before or after you introduce yourself, you will approach the accompanist with your sheet music, remembering to bring them a clean, unmarked copy, preferably in an easy to handle 3-ring notebook (double-sided pages or inserted in low-glare plastic sleeves). They will ask you what tempo you would like to sing the song, and generally, if you just sing the first measure or so for them very quietly (without them playing for you—although you can ask for your starting note to be played at that moment), they will be able to figure out how fast or slow you would like to take the song.

Then you go back to the spot in front of the director or folks listening to the audition, smile, take a deep breath, motion to the accompanist that you are ready and then, as the Nike ad says, "Just do it."

Typically in one of these auditions, you want to look just over their heads, so that you aren't distracted by anything they are doing. This is also sort of standard audition practice in a theatrical setting. Just so you are aware, they may start writing stuff at some point while you are singing. Don't let this throw you off. They need to take notes about you so that when the audition process is over and everyone has had their turn, they can go back and review their notes for casting purposes.

At the end of the audition, they will often just say, thank you. Do not be offended by this lack of feedback, it is standard practice. If they do want to talk with you some more, they will take the initiative to engage you and ask at that point.

In terms of choir auditions, the director will often tell you what he or she would like you to sing when you are making your email or phone inquiry. If it is something a bit out of your range, or that you are not comfortable with, talk with them honestly. Let them know you are just beginning and have never auditioned before. They will usually bend over backwards to have new choir members, and I know several friends who are choral directors who are willing to have folks sing something as simple as "Mary Had a Little Lamb" or "Row, Row, Row Your Boat."

No matter what, it is going to be scary the first time you do an audition. There is no way around that. But, if you can, for a brief moment, feel the fear and then reinterpret that energy as excitement about an opportunity to do something new in your life, you may notice that there is a similar feeling to the two energies. Always choose to be excited about what might come from your willingness to step out of your comfort zone. Perhaps it won't work the first time, but it is guaranteed that your perseverance and hard work training your voice will pay off.

And if I were to add one piece to this information that can help you with the singing and at the same time help you with your audition, it would be this: always remember to smile, and remember that they want to like you and your performance!

Staying Calm in the Midst of Chaos: Remembering To Breathe

Whenever we are about to do something totally new, something we have never experienced before, there are usually a variety of feelings associated with stepping out and taking that risk. Some words we might use to describe risk would include scary, uncertain, fearful, and out of control. These are normal sensations, and will only dissipate once the toes are in the water and we know what to expect.

So, how do we take positive action towards something we would really like to do, such as join a choir, sing at a coffee shop, participate in an open mic evening or do a musical, when our nerves might just want to stop us before we even get to the door?

Well, for me preparation handles some of the energy. Practice your song so that you know it really well, and even consider singing it in front of a supportive friend or two prior to stepping out into the world. Support is key here. Lots of people have the belief that not only can't they sing, but most everyone around them, as well. You do not need someone with negative opinions about your singing communicating to you at this stage of the game. Certainly, if they are kind and objective and suggest things that feel good to you, do that. But if all they want to do is pick you apart, find a friend who will support you with your vision. No negative thoughts—is important when we are trying to break through to a new level of creativity.

Once you have practiced and perhaps sung for someone else, you will know when you are ready to step out and make the next move. I wish that I could reach across this book and protect you from every possible negative situation that exists in this artistic realm. Unfortunately, you and I both know that the world is full of challenges, and unconscious people can be part of that reality. You may step out and get your feelings hurt, someone might not choose you or you might not get the part you wanted. But here's the deal— just by taking the chance and doing something brave, you empower yourself no matter what the final outcome.

Risking nothing creates nothing. Risking hurt and what-ifs creates immense possibilities, and will move you forward in life, no matter what the results are. There is a famous saying about how life is about the journey, not the destination. In this endeavor it is really a truism. Personally, I am proud of you just because you picked up this book. You took a chance. By opening it and working hard at understanding some new concepts, you found your singing voice. So, when it comes to finding your niche out in the world, take some time and research vocal groups that you might like to be a part of.

For example, I have been working with barbershop choruses and quartets. There is a huge resurgence of Sweet Adeline (SAI), Harmony, Inc., and Barbershop Harmony Society (BHS) choruses across the country. They are always looking for new singers and many of them provide coaching and training for their members, in order to continue to improve their group quality of sound.

If you go to www.sweetadelineintl.org, www.barbershop.org (men), or www.harmonyinc.org (women), you can learn more about these organizations and locate a chorus near you. Don't hesitate to contact any of these groups, as they are very open to new members. My experience with the entire barbershop world is that it not only offers a wonderful singing experience, but you are very likely to find new lifelong friends!

By preparing yourself and identifying the type of experience you are looking for, you will find your outlet for singing. A church choir is often a good supportive place to start, a larger community choir may be a possibility and then there's the barbershop option or local musical theater productions. One other avenue that can be fun is the classic Karaoke evening out with friends. It can be silly and not everyone sings perfectly, but who cares—it is about making a joyful noise and letting out some of that energy, while allowing that part of you that would really like to have a voice in this world claim a little bit of it with a microphone and sometimes cheesy accompaniment!

So again, the most important piece to remember is that you matter, and your voice matters. Take a deep breath and when the chaos of the world tries to press on you as you bravely walk forward with your new found voice, just remember that it is all about creating a safe place within ourselves to let our voices sing. Try not to fight the learning, no matter what that may look like, for as we learn, we grow, and as we grow we become even more of our true selves.

Chapter 11: Some Final Thoughts

Chapter 11: Some Final Thoughts

Finding the Right Teacher or Coach for You

The last piece of the puzzle is to help you identify the kind of voice teacher or coach that is going to be most appropriate for you. I am very partial to teachers that have a real understanding of the language issues, a strong comprehension of the musculature, and have at least some experience as singers themselves. Not that a coach has to be a singer: my master teacher really wasn't one, but I think he was the exception to the rule. He had a very good teacher himself, Dean Verhines, and had observed this man at U.C.L.A. working with many, many students as his primary accompanist, before he was qualified to take over that studio environment.

So, researching teachers in your area is a good first step, because having another set of ears to listen to you is very helpful in creating quicker results. Cost can be a factor; voice teachers tend to be more expensive than vocal coaches, but you may get less technical support from a coach than someone that actually teaches vocal production. Some coaches are really only interested in coaching repertoire, which means that they stay away from dealing with vocal technique challenges, unless it is something that can be fixed through the music.

I have put up several clips on YouTube.com at debralynnvocalcoach that are helpful to look at, because you can see and experience how I work. There will be information at the end of this book as to how you can work with me, via Skype sessions privately or through PowHow.com in a group setting online.

If you are interested in auditioning for shows like American Idol, America's Got Talent or X Factor, you will eventually want to work with someone one-on-one in order to help increase your success factor. In these particular cases, you may be able to check and see if anyone in your area has a proven track record with singers who have auditioned successfully for these shows. As my teacher always said, if you want to know whether a teacher is good or not, look at whether his or her singers are singing well.

But, if you are someone who has held the belief that you couldn't sing well yourself, you really need a coach who is emotionally supportive, understands vocal production, includes effective breath support and who wants to coach you; someone that you feel comfortable with and who, after a few sessions, you are able to look up and see some results. If you have been with a teacher for more than four to six sessions and you are not experiencing any positive results, you may be with the wrong person.

Not everyone is effective for everyone. Our personalities are different and we all have different ways of learning, some more kinesthetic and others audio or visual. Always trust your instincts—if something hurts, it is wrong, whether I am saying it or someone else is saying it.

So, now I need to add one more caveat, as we have shared a specific vocal journey together. Every teacher teaches differently, every single one. I had six teachers over a twenty-year period. My first got me started in high school. I was young and undisciplined, but I have always had fond memories of her, because she gave me support and encouragement at a time when I really needed it.

The four between her and my master teacher, Edward Sayegh, are a total blur with the exception of a University professor that did quite a bit of damage with me, in retrospect. Her communication that I should give up classical studies in voice because I would never be heard in a large concert hall was a falsehood, and had me leave my studies for a period of years. Of course, when I got to Edward and he explained resonance to me and how it all worked (as well as aired some annoyance regarding her evaluation), I was able to blow that belief out of the water.

To this day, I will never forget standing on a stage in front of the Maui Symphony Orchestra to a sold-out house of 1200 seats in the Maui Arts & Cultural Center's Castle Theatre, singing the Soprano solo sections of Handel's *Messiah*, feeling my voice fill the hall and thinking that every single precious moment of the four years that I spent with Edward was nothing less than priceless!

Our Emotional Body: Issues of Trauma and Singing with Ease

People magazine's March 8, 2010 issue featured an article about Susan Boyle and her emotional challenges associated with her sudden rise to fame. Her rendition of "I Dreamed a Dream" stunned Simon Cowell—not an easy thing to do in his world of talent competitions. I remember watching her sing that night on *Britain's Got Talent* and finding myself crying. Perhaps it was her story: a woman who had hidden herself from life and whose voice gave her the courage to step out onto that stage and share that voice with the world that touched me.

Recently, I was sharing with a friend my beliefs about the emotional body, and how it can impact our ability to release our voices, both in speaking and in singing. As a voice teacher, my primary objective is to help a student use their voice more effectively, and sometimes that is just a matter of technical adjustment. However, more often than not, issues of abuse, miscommunication, fear, and self-consciousness manifest in vocal challenges that directly affect a person's ability to release his or her voice in song. Over the years, a number of students studying with me have shared their abuse-related issues: physical or emotional abuse associated with family dysfunction, alcoholism and drug abuse, and even violence in the form of rape. Upon occasion when these students are open to alternative healing options, I have incorporated *Reiki* treatments into the voice studio. The energy of Reiki allows for deep healing to occur without the engagement of the mind, and I have been a practitioner since 1998. In each case, there has been an almost instantaneous shift in the students' vocalizing as the Reiki energy has been initiated in the session. Some of the ways this has manifested have included sudden freedom of sound, release of pain that has been held in the throat or head area, and opening of the ribs and ease of breath movement.

In addition to good vocal coaching, sometimes other healing modalities are helpful in assisting us to free our voices. Rolfing or massage can be helpful when there is tightness in the ribcage or when the ribs need to be opened up for more effective breathing. Feldenkreis work has often been touted to assist with the body's flexibility and posture; yoga also provides these benefits, and Pilates is great for your core and ability to sustain the rib control we have been discussing. Dance can also be helpful with posture and, if you are planning on auditioning for a musical theater production at some point, a little jazz or tap dance training is great.

I believe that everyone can sing, but sometimes, just one thought will get in the way of a person being able to sing with ease. Thoughts like, I can't sing, I'm not sure of the pitch, or that note is too high, normally occur right before the student articulates a sound, and in a split-second the voice is directed down a path of doubt toward almost certain vocal disaster.

As we have discussed throughout this book, doubt is one of the most dangerous thoughts, as it never creates a positive result! By disciplining our minds and recognizing when these thoughts sneak in, we can, in essence, stop the chatter and focus on the things that will help us create a great sound.

Susan Boyle was a miraculous presence for us to witness, as her life's story would indicate that she wasn't imbued with great self-confidence and as her brothers have shared, she was challenged by circumstances surrounding fame.

But even for those of us who never want to sing in public, our ability to sing with a sense of freedom, even in the shower, can be determined by the beliefs that lie deep within us. Releasing those fears, concerns or judgments can, in a single moment, release our voices from self-imposed prisons of thought and allow for the possibility of singing with ease, bringing new meaning to the phrase, "Make a joyful noise...!"

This is the bottom line for all of us. When we are no longer under the negative effects of constriction, tension, vowel placement, support issues and breath control, an opening is created for effortless sound. Sure, we are thinking like crazy at times and engaging our bodies to get underneath the sound, but without the pain and struggle, our ability to express ourselves through our voices is made manifest with incredible freedom.

It is my mission and vision to help as many singers as I can in my lifetime to experience the joy of effortless, well-tuned, consistent singing. With all the stress we face in our lives, and in a world that sometimes feels out of control, to be able to express one's own personality and heart through the voice is a great gift that not only eases tension, but makes people smile!

You will often hear me say, "Keep the lift!" This energy that is stabilized in the Buzz zone will change your life. It changed mine, and the gratitude I have for the learning, the support and all the love I have received, both on stage and off, is undeniable and unending. Thank you to all my teachers, but most especially to Edward. My heart will always be with him. I must admit he worked me very hard, but he gave me the one thing I had always dreamed of—a career in music. Perhaps it didn't look like either one of us expected, but it has unfolded in a beautiful Divine way.

Chapter 11: Some Final Thoughts

In my heart of hearts I believe my voice was a gift from God. I chose to take responsibility for its care, and now I feel incredibly privileged to share that which has been bestowed on me, with you. May you find your own vocal ease through understanding how the voice works, for it seems to me that this world needs every last one of us singing our own unique and well-tuned song!

Appendix:

The Barbershop and *Bel Canto* Connection

My dad was a barbershopper. During the 1960s and 1970s, he sang baritone in two barbershop choruses, The Coastmen, in South Florida under the tutelage of one of the barbershop world's most famous quartets, The Suntones, and in the Silk City Chorus, under the baton of the late Vin Zito in Manchester, Connecticut.

Throughout my childhood, the recordings of The Suntones were almost constantly playing in the background. To this day, I remember going to Bushnell Auditorium each year for a men's barbershop concert, and each time feeling the beauty and power of this truly American musical style. The unique barbershop ring, a fifth harmonic tone created by the straight-tone, four part harmony, is what makes this particular style of music unique.

As a young person I was immersed in this sound, but at the time, I did not have a direct interest in singing the style myself. My path seemed to direct me toward classical vocal understanding, something which, at the time, my father seemed somewhat perplexed about. He regularly tried to communicate that all I needed to do was to "put my hands in my pockets and sing!" This, of course, is not a bad idea at all, but I wanted to understand the voice and be able to have control of my instrument, so that I could be a professional.

Almost thirty years later, my training in bel canto and my experience with barbershop collided once again. Having relocated to Middlebury, Vermont, I was embraced as a vocal production coach for a group of forty-five women, who just happened to sing barbershop style music—Maiden Vermont. Their director, Lindi Bortney, had visited Maui where I was teaching earlier that year and observed the rapid results created in my private studio with one of her singers.

Appendix:

In an inspired moment, she declared that it would be wonderful if sometime I could come coach her gals. Within six months, that opportunity manifested. It led to an amazing discovery, which has directed my footsteps back into my father's world of barbershop music.

Together, we discovered that the demands of barbershop mimic the demands of bel canto. The same requirement of pure, vowel, forward placement, combined with an elongated need for beyond average breath control and sustainment of straight-tone or limited vibrato, allow for the dovetail between this American style of music with this specific classical approach to vocal production.

Probably the biggest challenge barbershop singers face is accurate intonation. This is due to the fact that without absolute pitch accuracy in each of the four parts, the desired fifth note in the overtone series does not consistently lock and sound, or as barbershoppers say, "ring!" As you now well know, the Americanized-English language compounds our intonation issues and, without this understanding, much of our singing goes out of tune.

The Barbershop Harmony Society (BHS), Sweet Adeline's International (SAI) and Harmony, Inc., are all organizations which primarily draw amateur singers. Over the years, the level of competency has increased, creating a highly competitive spin on the top medals and putting pressure on those singers without training to increase their individual skills. Now the demand for techniques to keep supported, in-tune singing becomes paramount to high-level contest placement.

After ten months of in-house coaching in Vermont, the extraordinary results produced with this large group of beginning singers was apparent to both the director, Lindi Bortney, a thirty-three year veteran of SAI, and me. These gals had enthusiastically applied all the musculature principles, including expanded ribs and limited airflow, and incorporated the forward-vowel production in such a way that the intonation issue was completely negated.

No longer were syllables sagging or closing too soon; *legato* lines were strengthened throughout each of the four parts; section sound was unified through the usage of the same target vowel sounds; and this wonderful group of women were freed up to do what they really wanted to do most—make beautiful music. At this point, there were no individual vocal issues holding back the artistic expression that is so much a part of this style of music. When Lindi said, "You're my secret weapon! Thank you for giving me the chorus of my dreams!" I knew I had done my job.

Within a year of this collaboration, I was published in a series of two articles (Nov/Dec 2010 and Jan/Feb 2011) called, "Sing Like An Italian" in *The Harmonizer,* the Men's Barbershop Harmony Society trade magazine. This has led to coaching with choruses and quartets throughout the United States of America and Canada. The superior results created with the bel canto understanding are being felt worldwide.

Appendix:

Warm-Up Recommendations

Now that you have a great idea of how the singing musculature and process works physically, visit my website at www.debralynnmusic.com to register for a free "Phlegm is Your Friend" video exercise clip and order a copy of either my Men's or Women's instructional Warm-Ups. All ages can use these exercises, which are available on CD and also in digital download format. My exercises are designed to align the voice from the bottom of your chest register to the top of your head register (or for men, falsetto register), helping to stabilize your forward and inner lifts, as well as smooth out your passaggios and give you your entire vocal range…with ease!

In combination with the principles learned here, these exercises will get you off to a great start towards discovering your balanced, beautiful voice! The CD breaks the process down for better integration, by working one piece of the puzzle at a time, and includes introduction instructional tracks to remind you of the specific preparation and lifts, as we discover and anchor our *Bel Canto Buzz*!

As I mentioned earlier, you can find some basic vocal production videos on my YouTube.com site at debralynnvocalcoach. These are great for getting you started and you will be able to see examples of my exercises and dialogues to better understand your voice.

Skype and PowHow.com (www.powhow.com/classes/bel-canto-buzz) are two other ways to continue this work with online support. If you go to my website, you will be able to email me for more information. I would love to assist you in finding your own unique balanced instrument, and believe that the magic offered through bel canto understanding is nothing short of miraculous. It certainly has been a miracle in my life.

On the day I felt effortless singing, my life changed. Not only did I get to manifest my dream of becoming a professional singer, but also

Appendix:

through this path I've been directed to my life's work—assisting others to sing with ease!

There is nothing more profound than watching transformation in action. For over twenty years, I've seen a plethora of emotions: tears, joy, glee, hope, and great sighs of relief. Many, many people have opened their hearts to me all around the world and enriched my life through their faith and trust in my ability to help them to find their own beautiful voice. I never, ever take this blessed gift for granted.

My own singing has brought so much joy to my life. It is a well-known fact that music has the ability to transform lives. Singing has the ability to transform yours!

Let's get our *Bel Canto*—beautiful singing—*Buzz* on together, shall we?!

Glossary—Debra's Casual Explanation of Musical Terms

Ballad—A slower, more legato song

Bel canto—An Italian term that means beautiful singing.

Crescendo—Becoming louder, swelling, increasing energy and leaning in

Decrescendo—Becoming softer, diminishing, pulling back on energy with intention

Dotted note—Increases the value of the note attached to by one half.

E.N.T.—Ear, nose and throat doctor

Frontal Lift—Where the cheek muscles are engaged and lifted off of the gum line.

Forte—Loud

Inner Smile—A way of stabilizing the soft palate in the upright position.

Interval—The distance between two notes on the scale.

Key Signature—The number of flats or sharps that are used in any given piece of music.

Laryngeal Reflux—Occurs when stomach acids find their way back up to the larynx, often without feeling the symptoms of typical acid reflux or heartburn.

Legato—In Italian, legato means line; implies smooth and connected.

Measure—One segment of time, when combined with other measures makes up a song.

Mezzo Forte—Medium loud

Nodules—The equivalent of calluses on the larynx or vocal folds.

Note values (quarter, half, whole...)—A length of time a note is held.

Octave—From one note up eight more (i.e., C to C, B to B, A to A and so forth)

Pianissimo—Soft, intense not whispered

Appendix:

Passaggio—An Italian word that means passageway; the transition between vocal registers.

Polyps—A tab-like growth on the larynx or vocal folds.

Register—Areas of the voice associated with different resonating areas (chest, middle, head, falsetto)

Staff—The lines on music paper where notes are written for the voice or instrument.

Tempo—The speed at which a song is sung.

Time Signature—Defines how many notes to a measure. (Ex.: 4/4 time = 4 quarter notes)

Up-Tempo—A quick or lively song sometimes referred to as a patter song.

Acknowledgments

Without the assistance of many, many people I would have not experienced success in my singing career or in writing this book. Six years of work have gone into these pages, every single one of them filled with my love for the craft of singing and the people I get to work with daily.

To Edward Sayegh, my bel canto Maestro, there are almost no words. After my college professor said that I should give up classical music because I would never be heard in a hall, you championed me for four years. Your understanding of the bel canto of Manuel Garcia and Mathilde Marchese helped transform me into who I am today. I will always be grateful and recognize that without you, none of this work would be happening.

To Daniel Lockert, my first professional accompanist and coach, you taught me about partnership and what it means to be a musical team player. These skills have spilled into all of my understanding and impact my life and work every day. Thank you!

Thank you to Elaine Cissi, Richard Bowering, Shannon Miles, Susan Arnold, Georgia Hughes, Kelley Mairson-Hutchison, Gretchen Adamek, Jennifer Winston, and Debbie Fortier-Carone for your editorial feedback (and friendship) and to Sam Horn for seeing the possibility of me making a larger contribution to the world, back in 2005.

Thank you to Ray Charbonneau for walking me through the perils of self-publishing and assisting in the formatting of this book, both for those of us who still like to hold a copy of a real book, and those who would prefer to upload it onto their e-book device!

Thank you to Sally Foster for the playful internal illustrations, to Kendra Weber Gratton for the inspired Gondolier, and to Ken Martin for creating the wonderful cover. Your love of art and sense of humor have brought this book to life!

To my Mom and Dad, Mary Jo and George Mount, thank you for all your years of emotional support and financial investment in my voice, it sure was a pretty penny! These vocal cords are literally worth more than their weight in gold. Dad, thank you for instilling in me a love of barbershop harmony. All those years of listening to ringing chords gave me my musical ear, which is now assisting so many people to sing with ease in four-part harmony. Love you both!

To Jerry Eiting, many heartfelt thanks for being the singing partner I always dreamed of having. Your brilliant baritone and easy-going demeanor inspired me to reach higher and work harder to make beautiful music. From the stage of the Historic Iao Theater in Wailuku as Lancelot and Guinevere to our 12-years together culminating on the beautiful Castle Theater stage at the Maui Arts & Cultural Center, your presence gave me courage to realize my dream of being a professional singer. If I close my eyes I can still remember the profound comfort I felt standing next to you backstage, the very first time, as we prepared to make our entrance. Mahalo nui loa!

To Stuart Funke-d'Egnuff, thank you for all the years of support and love. Your vision of who I could be still urges me onward. Everything I understand about mastery and empowerment, I learned from you.

Many, many thanks to Stephen Haines, Danny Brown and Anne Durham for accompanying me so beautifully during my time on Maui; as well as to Vania Jerome, whose own bel canto legacy bonded us as sisters in song from the very start; to Curt Lee for helping me record my first Christmas album and to Joel Katz for arranging and engineering *Heaven in Your Heart*, a project for which I will always be proud.

A big *mahalo* to Walter Bissett, Sarah Oppenheim-Beggs and Bob Wills for taking my vision for Maui Civic Light Opera (MCLO) and continuing its legacy with Musical Voices Maui. I'm forever grateful for your continued dedication to beautiful music and the empowerment of others on the beautiful island of Maui. To Richard Cray and the cast of *Phantom*, and MAPA, you all made one of my most precious dreams come true. Thank you for standing beside me for that year, as we made magic!

Today, my deepest thanks goes to Lindi Bortney, whose faith in me assisted me to transition one of the most challenging periods of my life. Your willingness to share your platform in the realm of vocal production for almost a year and trust my work with your precious Maiden Vermont ladies was a profound gift. Your love for me and for the gifts I bring, set me on a serendipitous path that seemingly has no end. The contribution our research together will make in the world of barbershop harmony, I believe will ring on for years to come.

Many thanks to Brent Graham for spending an hour and a half watching my YouTube.com videos and calling me to talk about my work. You got the whole ball rolling for bel canto within the Men's International Barbershop Harmony Society!

To my very dear friend and colleague, Kate Michaels—Your own beautiful voice has taken you on a grand journey. I've always been so proud of you. Your friendship has consistently and lovingly supported and guided me, all the way back to our time together in Edward's studio in San Francisco. I'm grateful for your belief in me, as a person, singer, teacher and spiritual presence.

And finally, thank you to the hundreds of students that I have been privileged to work with over the years. My memories of our work together suffuse these pages and I will forever hold each of you in my heart. Thank you for sharing your lives and voices with me, for you

Acknowledgments

have inspired every word in *The Bel Canto Buzz: Beautiful Singing Made Simple!*

About the Author

Since graduating with her B. A. in Voice Performance and a minor in Arts Administration from Florida State University and the College of Charleston, Debra Lynn has lived and performed around the world — Palm Beach, Denver, San Francisco, Honolulu, Maui, Austria, Germany, France, Ireland, and Scotland. A professional singer since 1998, Debra has performed as principle soprano with the Maui and Honolulu Symphony Orchestras, shared the stage with Viennese Operatic tenor Sir John van Kesteren and the legendary Jim Nabors, and has opened for Marianne Williamson, Wayne Dyer and Ram Dass. In 2009, her first original CD, Heaven in Your Heart, was a finalist for Inspirational Album of the Year for the Na Hoku Hanohano Awards.

Prior to her four-year post-graduate intensive with bel canto master teacher, Edward Sayegh, Debra was trained in individual and group empowerment within the human potential movement. Imbued with a deep sense of service, she has melded these communication skills with time-honored bel canto technical understanding and her loving sense of humor hard-earned through rigorous life lessons, to assist thousands of people to achieve true vocal and emotional freedom.

Debra's daily mission is to break up belief systems of the mind, direct attention to the vocal instrument that each of us contains within, gently reconnect the heart to the process and allow for the magical manifestation of one's own unique voice, using the pathway laid before us by the scientific and artistic discoveries of Manuel Garcia and Mathilde Marchesi almost 200 years ago.

About the Author

Debra resides in New England, where she has two grown sons, loves to be outdoors walking or snuggled up by a fire, writing, songwriting, reading, needlepointing, daydreaming and generally contemplating getting into some sort of mischief...

Interested in publishing your own book?

Ray Charbonneau can help you design and publish your book quickly, professionally, and at a low cost. Unlike other services that automate the process, Ray will work directly with you every step of the way to ensure you get the book you want.

For more information, visit the Y42K Book Production Services page at:

http://www.y42k.com/bookproduction.html

Made in the USA
San Bernardino, CA
07 April 2015